PUPPY TRAINING FAST TRACK EASY STEP-BY-STEP GUIDE FOR THE FIRST WEEKS AT HOME

SIT, STAY, RELEASE, RECALL, CRATE, POTTY & ANXIETY WITH RESULTS TRACKERS FOR FAST RESULTS

HELEN DEVLIN

CONTENTS

INTRODUCTION

This hands-on puppy training guide focuses on practical actions and solutions. For that reason it is partly designed as a guide or workbook. This means that it can help you tackle puppy training step-by-step, but it will also serve as a cherished keepsake of your puppy's first adventures!

Sometimes we simply need to get the point of exactly what are required to do, and how, rather than understanding the reasoning behind it all.

This book is structured very much like a checklist, with exercises and places where you can record your puppy's progress. The intention is not only to train your puppy but to also remind you to pay attention to what they are trying to tell you.

We will start at the very beginning - and many of you will already have been through the choosing your pup part - before going through the basic training of mouthing and house training, then we will go on to cover the basic cues of sit, stay and release. We also show you how to crate train your puppy, before moving on to the slightly more advanced training of leash and recall as well as separation anxiety.

I have tried to keep this a simple and as easy as possible but I would also like to add that one of the best ways to train your puppy is to use body signals as early as possible. In all of the following exercises, think of a hand signal that you can use and, ideally, begin with signals even before you start using word cues. If you need more information on this there are details of a free course at the end of the book. It's not essential, but it might help you understand your puppy a little bit better.

Enjoy this magical phase and, now, let's get to work!

1

PREPARING FOR YOUR PUPPY - CHECK LIST

This chapter deals with all the things that you need to have prepared in advance of your puppy's arrival. For that reason, it is very much a shopping list of to-do's and reminders. We'll start the training in the next chapter.

CHOOSING YOUR PUPPY

By this point you may already have chosen your puppy (congratulations!), but for those who are almost there we have a few reminders of what you might want to consider because, often, the success of your puppy journey starts with selecting the right breed. You will no doubt have already thought about your lifestyle, living situation, and long-term commitment.

The point that is most often forgotten, is the exercise needs of different breeds - and often bigger dogs won't need as much exercise as some smaller dog types. Greyhounds and Spaniels spring to mind here.

As you begin your preparations begin don't forget to bear in mind:

- Space requirements for your chosen breed at full size
- Exercise needs and your available time
- Grooming requirements and associated costs
- Breed-specific health considerations
- Local breed restrictions or housing regulations

Bringing a new puppy home is exciting but it requires some planning too – especially the often-forgotten safety precautions around the home and garden.

This chapter will simply list the essential steps to create a safe, welcoming home for your new family member.

TIMELINE: 1-2 WEEKS BEFORE ARRIVAL

Proper preparation can take time. Try to cover these essential tasks at least 2 weeks before your puppy arrives to ensure everything is ready.

FINDING A VETERINARIAN

Establishing a relationship with a trusted veterinarian is one of the things we often don't think about but it really can make a big difference for your puppy's health.

If at all possible, try to find and independent vet rather than one owned by a Venture Capital Fund or large organization. Google can be your friend here too, so once you have found a vet, do some research on them and try to find honest reviews. For some of you, you will need to begin your search early to ensure availability for your puppy's first checkup.

- Seek recommendations from local dog owners as well as online research
- Prioritize independent veterinary practices over corporate chains if you can

- Schedule an initial puppy check-up before arrival
- Get emergency vet contact information

ESSENTIAL SUPPLIES (WITH APPROXIMATE BUDGET)

You are going to need some essentials and most of them are pretty obvious - but you would be surprised how many of us forget the basics like a dog bowl because we are so involved in finding the prefect bed. It goes without saying that a well-equipped home can really help your puppy adjust quickly.

This list covers everything you'll need, organized by category and purpose.

Basic Equipment

- Crate sized for adult dog weight ($40-120)
- A basket or bed (especially of you are not using a crate) or a puppy bed that fits inside crate ($20-40)
- Food and water bowls, stainless steel recommended ($10-30)
- Collar with ID tag and 4-6ft leash ($15-30)
- Baby gates for restricted areas ($25-50 each)
- Grooming supplies (brush, shampoo, nail clippers) - these will be useful slightly later and don't need to be bought in advance.

Care Items

- High-quality puppy food specific to breed size ($20-50)
- Training treats ($10-15)
- Enzymatic cleaner for potty accidents ($10-20). This is a cleaning product that uses enzymes to break down and remove organic matter, such as stains, and odors. For example Nature's Miracle Dog Stain and Odor Remover is available for around $11 per 32-ounce bottle.

- Basic grooming supplies (brush, puppy shampoo) ($30-50)

Toys

- 2-3 sturdy chew toys (avoid plush toys initially) ($20-30)
- Puzzle toys for mental stimulation ($15-30)
- Kong or similar fillable toy ($10-15) - an essential item for separation anxiety

HOME PREPARATION CHECKLIST

Puppy-proofing your home prevents accidents and creates a safe environment for exploration. Follow these room-by-room guidelines to secure your space.

Puppy Zone Requirements

- Quiet area away from household traffic
- Easy-to-clean flooring
- Temperature-controlled environment
- Access to designated potty area
- Space for crate, bed, and play area

ROOM-BY-ROOM PUPPY PROOFING GUIDE

Kitchen

- Install childproof latches on under-sink cabinets containing cleaning supplies
- Secure trash can with locking lid
- Store food in airtight containers above counter height
- Keep cleaning supplies and chemicals in high cabinets
- Remove access to dishwasher

- Shield electrical cords from appliances
- Store sharp utensils in drawers with safety latches

Living Room

- Tape down or cover electrical cords
- Remove or secure unstable furniture
- Protect corners of coffee tables
- Move fragile items to high shelves
- Secure TV and entertainment center
- Remove toxic houseplants (see the examples at the end of the book)
- Cover electrical outlets
- Secure window blind cords

Bathroom

- Keep toilet lid closed (install lock if needed)
- Store medications in secure cabinet
- Keep cleaning supplies in high cabinets
- Store personal care items (razors, cotton swabs) out of reach
- Keep trash can behind closed door
- Store toilet paper on holders, not floor

Bedroom

- Store shoes in closets
- Keep laundry in closed hampers
- Secure drawers containing clothing
- Remove or secure hanging clothes
- Keep jewelry and small items in boxes
- Store phone chargers safely

Laundry Room

- Keep detergents on high shelves
- Secure washer and dryer doors
- Install childproof latches on cabinets
- Check behind machines for exposed wires
- Keep dryer sheets out of reach
- Store cleaning tools (mops, brooms) in closed closet

Home Office

- Secure loose cables and wires
- Keep paper clips, pens and rubber bands stored
- Lock file cabinets containing supplies
- Protect computer cables
- Store books on secure shelves
- Keep desk drawers closed
- Remove access to paper shredders

Garage

- Store automotive fluids on high shelves
- Secure tools in locked cabinets
- Keep paint and chemicals locked away
- Remove access to workbenches
- Store garden supplies safely
- Check for antifreeze leaks regularly

Outdoor Areas

- Check fence integrity weekly
- Remove toxic plants
- Secure garden tools
- Cover pools/ponds
- Store chemicals in locked shed
- Remove mushrooms promptly

- Check for escape routes under gates

FIRST DAYS AT HOME

1. Set up a designated space for your puppy with their bed, crate, and toys.
2. Decide on the outdoor place where you want your puppy to toilet.
3. Introduce your puppy to family members and other pets gradually.
4. Decide on the outdoor place where you want your puppy to toilet.
5. Give them time to sleep - remember, they need a lot of sleep!
6. Stick to a routine to help your puppy feel secure.

You will want all of the family involved in his early training and you need to think about this before he arrives. Work out who can do what and try and get all your household members on board as early as you can (this is also good for helping to prevent separation anxiety). You might want to try and get agreement on who does the morning, or lunch or evening care or who's job it is to think up a game to play on a particular day.

And don't forget to pick the name of your puppy!

INTERACTIVE CHECKLIST

Anticipate and prepare for typical adjustment issues. These solutions will help you handle common challenges over the first few days and weeks and we will talk about them in the following chapters.

Common First Week Challenges

- Night crying: Solutions and management
- Feeding schedule adjustments
- Potty training basics
- Crate training introduction
- Managing puppy biting

Monitor your puppy's progress and maintain important records with the practical worksheets and checklists contained in this book – it's a great starter pack to get you in the habit.

And don't forget to note down contact information for you veterinary and keep it where everyone can find it!

RECORD

Vet contact: _____

Breed chosen: _____

Date of puppy's arrival: _____

First vet appointment date: _____

Designated potty area: _____

Tracking Progress

Date	Task	Completed (Yes/No)	Notes
	Choose a breed		
	Purchase supplies		
	Puppy-proofing		
	Set up sleeping area		
	Establish potty routine		

2

YOUR PUPPY'S FIRST WEEK HOME: SETTING UP FOR SUCCESS

Bringing your puppy home is incredibly exciting, but remember - your little one has just left everything they've ever known including their familiar environment, siblings, and mother. Gentle introductions and calm energy will help your puppy feel secure in their new world.

Socialization Planning

Early socialization shapes your puppy's future behavior and it can start as soon as your puppy arrives home but you need to avoid any dogs that you don't know and dogs that are not vaccinated and don't let your puppy on the ground in any areas where any other dogs toilet. Your aim is to use this period wisely to create positive associations with new experiences. We have more about socialization in the chapter on Separation Anxiety.

Create a positive exposure checklist

- Create a positive exposure checklist
- Different floor surfaces

- Various sounds (traffic, appliances)
- Meeting vaccinated dogs
- Encountering different people
- Car rides
- Basic handling exercises

WHAT YOU NEED FROM THE BREEDER

Before you bring your puppy to his forever home, you need to find out what type of food your puppy has been eating up until this point. Your breeder will be happy to let you know and should provide you with a starter pack of what they have been feeding him. Don't worry if they don't do this as standard practice, just make sure that you know what you need to have in the house for the arrival of your new puppy.

You will introduce him to the food you want to use slowly by mixing some of his existing food into the new food that you have chosen. Slowly increase the proportion of his new food over a period of 7-10 days. You also need to know how often he was being fed, and at what time because, initially, you will stick to this pattern and gradually change it if you need to do so.

You do this because any sudden change to his diet will upset his tummy. It will make him feel uncomfortable and can result in unexpected accidents caused by diarrhoea which your puppy won't be able to control. It simply makes it more difficult to successfully start potty training in these first few important days.

As you start to slowly change over his food you can also start to gradually change the time at which he gets his food so that the schedule moves to the times that works within your household.

If you need to change his food at any point in his life then you will always repeat the process of gradually mixing in the old food with the new. Dogs - and their stomachs - don't like a sudden change to their diet so always remember to introduce a new dog food slowly, no matter how old he is.

In order to get help him settle quickly in his new home you will need to make sure that you have something that smells familiar to him when he arrives. If the breeder doesn't have something you can take home with you, then ask if you can leave some clothing for him for a at least a week so that you can take it home with your puppy (a sock or an old towel will do).

Once he arrives home, put this item into the crate or basket that you want his to use. This will give your puppy some comfort over the first few days, and be a familiar smell which should help him settle in.

Finally, a reminder that, if you have a yard or garden, you will need to puppy-proof it. If there are any gaps in a fence or hedge, your puppy will find it, and he will disappear in a second to go exploring. You can use plastic chicken-wire or something similar but anything that will securely block access will do.

Don't forget that your puppy will want to chew things inside the home too, so you will need to puppy-proof any electrical wires (move them out of reach if you can) along with house-plants, some of which are poisonous to him.

THE JOURNEY HOME

Your puppy's first car ride can be nerve-wracking for them. Here's how to make it as stress-free as possible:

- Have someone sit beside them in the back seat - puppies love gentle reassurance
- Line the seat with puppy pads (trust me, accidents happen when we're nervous!)
- Keep the journey peaceful - save the celebratory music for later

- Drive straight home - your puppy needs to settle in before any adventures

Pro Tip: Bring a towel that smells of their mother/siblings - this familiar scent provides comfort during the journey.

FIRST HOURS AT HOME

These precious first hours set the tone for your future together and in this new world you are his tour guide. It is now that he will grow to trust you and look to you for guidance.

- Head straight to their designated toilet area - they'll likely need to go after the journey
- Introduce their special zone calmly - let them discover their bed and water bowl at their own pace
- Offer small amounts of water - excitement can lead to over-drinking
- Allow gentle exploration of their safe area - curiosity is good!
- Keep children seated and quiet - let the puppy approach them
- Respect their need for sleep - just like human babies, puppies need lots of rest to process new experiences

Remember: Less is more on day one. Your puppy doesn't need to meet the whole neighborhood just yet!

DAYS 2-3: ESTABLISHING ROUTINE

Now comes the fun part - helping your puppy learn about their new life through consistent, gentle routines.

Daily Schedule

Here's a schedule that works well for most puppies. Don't worry if you need to adjust it slightly for your situation - consistency matters more than perfect timing. We have a more detailed daily schedule in the chapter called House & Potty training.

6:00 AM - Good morning potty break (yes, puppies rise early!)

7:00 AM - Breakfast time followed by gentle play

8:00 AM - Another potty break (they'll need to go about 15 minutes after eating)

9:00 AM - Nap time (watch for signs like puppy grumpiness or excessive biting)

Smart Tip: Set alarms on your phone for the first few days - it helps you stay consistent while you're learning their patterns.

BUILDING TRUST THROUGH ROUTINE

These early days are all about helping your puppy feel secure:

- Feed at the same times each day - a hungry puppy is a grumpy puppy!
- Watch for their "I need to potty" dance - circling, sniffing, whining
- Use their name positively - never for scolding
- Practice gentle handling while they're calm - touch paws, ears, tail
- Let them explore safely - supervision is key

Handy Hint: Keep a notepad handy to track potty times, meals, and sleep patterns - you'll start seeing their natural rhythm emerge.

DAYS 4-5: BUILDING CONFIDENCE

By now, your puppy should be starting to feel more at home. Time to gently expand their world!

Structured Activities

These few days are your puppy's first steps into becoming a confident dog:

- Let them experience different floor surfaces and textures - tile, wood, carpet. Some puppies might be hesitant about new surfaces - that's perfectly normal! Make it fun by dropping tiny treats on different flooring.
- Introduce normal house noises gradually - the dishwasher, washing machine, vacuum (turned off initially). Keep experiences positive by pairing sounds with treats.
- Each family member gets quiet, gentle handling time. Think soft ear touches, gentle paw holds, sweet belly rubs - all while puppy is calm.
- Mini Grooming: Keep it brief and pleasant! Just 2 minutes of soft brushing, paired with treats. This builds foundation for future grooming.

Smart Tip: Watch your puppy's body language - a relaxed, wiggly puppy is ready for more, while one who moves away or freezes needs a break.

NORMAL VS CONCERNING BEHAVIOR

Normal Puppy Behaviors

- Brief crying at night (gradually decreasing)
- Playful nipping during games
- Short bursts of energy followed by deep sleep

- Occasional accidents despite regular potty trips
- Startling at new sounds then recovering quickly
- "Zoom" sessions before nap time

Signs Needing Attention

- Constant crying that increases over days
- Aggressive food guarding (growling, snapping)
- Hiding for long periods
- No interest in play or exploration
- Excessive fearfulness that doesn't improve
- Refusing meals (beyond initial adjustment)

DAYS 6-7: EXPANDING HORIZONS

Your puppy's confidence should be growing nicely now. Time for some structured fun!

Positive Activities

Garden Adventures: Short, supervised explorations. Let them sniff and discover - it's like reading the morning newspaper for dogs!

Collar Introduction: If not done earlier, start with short wearing periods. Turn any fussing into a game - treats and praise work wonders.

Name Game: Call their name in a happy voice, treat when they look. Soon they'll think their name means "good things happen!"

Play Sessions: Keep them short (5 minutes) and end while puppy still wants more. This builds drive for future training.

Pro Tip: Always end activities while puppy is successful and eager for more - this builds confidence and enthusiasm.

MAKING IT THROUGH COMMON CHALLENGES

Sleep Struggles

Almost every puppy has some sleep issues. Here's what helps:

- White noise machine or soft music
- Item carrying mother's scent
- Hot water bottle wrapped in blanket
- Creating dark, den-like environment
- Maintaining bedtime routine

Clever Hack: An old-fashioned ticking clock mimics mother's heartbeat!

Feeding Success

- Keep mealtimes consistent
- Use their regular food as rewards
- Monitor water intake (especially evening)
- Clean bowls daily
- Feed in same quiet location

Kitchen Tip: Measure daily food portions in morning - helps track intake.

Managing Alone Time

- Start tiny separations now to prevent future anxiety:
- Step out of sight briefly while puppy eats
- Move around house while puppy in safe zone
- No dramatic goodbyes or returns
- Gradually increase absence duration
- Keep departures and returns calm

The Biting Phase

All puppies bite - it's how they explore their world. We'll cover mouthing a chewing in more detail in the next chapter but here is a short summary.

- Redirect to appropriate toys
- Use soft yelp when they bite
- Praise gentle interactions
- End play if biting continues
- Ensure adequate sleep (overtired puppies bite more)

I want to highlight the need for sleep again, You puppy should be sleeping most of the day – in fact some puppies will sleep for over 18 hours. They need to sleep because it is important for their physical and mental health – it helps the muscles and brain develop. Make sure you make time for this and try to avoid too many eager visitors throughout the day and night. It is very hard to let a puppy sleep, especially in the first few days and weeks, but he really needs to.

YOUR FIRST WEEK TOOLKIT

Must-Have Items Within Reach

- Paper towels (lots!)
- Enzyme cleaner
- Treats in every room
- Favorite toys
- Puppy pads
- Quick-access vet number
- Camera for milestones
- Notebook for tracking

Daily Tracking Sheet

Keep notes on:

- Potty success/accidents
- Meal times/amounts
- Sleep patterns
- Energy levels
- New experiences (examples in interactive exercise)
- Medical observations

Celebrating Success

Remember to acknowledge the small wins:

- First night without crying
- Successfully using potty area
- Calm greetings
- Responding to name
- Settled nap times
- Playful interactions

- Confident exploration

Looking Ahead

By week's end, you should have:

- Established basic routine
- Started sleep pattern
- Built trust foundation
- Begun gentle handling
- Created safe experiences
- Documented health baseline

Take care of yourself too - a rested, patient human makes for a more confident puppy!

When to Call the Vet

While most first-week challenges are normal adjustment issues, some signs warrant professional attention:

- Refuses two meals in a row (puppies should be eager eaters!)
- Severe diarrhea (a bit of loose stool is normal with changes, but watch for frequent or watery stools)
- Unusual lethargy (puppies should have bursts of energy between naps)
- Continuous crying (beyond normal adjustment whimpers)
- Any blood in stool (even small amounts)
- Repeated vomiting
- Signs of dehydration (dry gums, lethargy, skin tenting)

Trust your instincts: It's better to make a precautionary call than wait too long. Most vets welcome new puppy questions!

Remember that perfect puppies don't exist - but perfectly normal puppies have ups and downs. Trust the process, stay consistent, and celebrate small victories. This week is about building trust, establishing routines, and helping your puppy feel secure. Everything else - training, socializing, perfect behavior - can wait. Focus on helping your new family member feel safe and loved in their forever home. This first week is all about laying the groundwork for a lifetime of joy together!

Final Tip: Take lots of photos - puppies grow incredibly fast, and you'll treasure these early memories!

INTERACTIVE CHECKLIST

Fill-in-the-Blank

Signs of happiness in my puppy:

_____

_____

_____

My puppy's reaction to new people:

_____

_____

_____

PRACTICE EXERCISES

1. First Night at Home

Describe your puppy's behavior during the first night.

Did they settle in easily? (Yes/No)

Any issues? Describe:

_____

_____

2. Observation Exercise

Spend 10 minutes observing your puppy and note their body language and behavior.

Date: _____

Behaviors observed:

_____

_____

3. Separation Anxiety Exercise

Practice leaving the room while your puppy is in the crate or carry-bag but don't secure the carry-bag or crate. It's very likely, that at this stage, your puppy will run out to follow you. That's ok.

Date: _____

Time spent out of sight (if any): _____

Success rate (if any): _____

Any signs of anxiety? (Yes/No) If yes, describe:

_____

_____

4. Introduce your puppy to a new person or dog

Date:

New experience: _____

Puppy's reaction:

_____

_____

5. Meeting a Stranger

Introduce your puppy to a stranger and note their behavior.

Steps taken: _____

Puppy's response:

_____

_____

6. Visiting a New House

Record your puppy's behavior during the visit.

New experiences encountered: _____

Puppy's reaction:

_____

_____

7. Note any places that your puppy goes to toilet and place a puppy pad there - note success e.g. place/s, puppy pad added, any problems/success

_____

_____

3
MOUTHING AND CHEWING

Your puppy's tiny teeth are remarkably sharp - and you'll soon discover this firsthand.

Mouthing is a natural behavior that puppies start from just a few weeks old. They 'mouth' to explore their world, learn about different textures, and develop crucial skills. We'll guide you through understanding and managing both mouthing and chewing behaviors, helping your puppy develop good habits while protecting your fingers (and furniture!).

UNDERSTANDING MOUTHING

Puppies mouth everything, including your hands, clothes, and ankles. This natural behavior helps them learn about their environment and develop bite inhibition - the ability to control their jaw pressure. Puppies who grow up with littermates often learn this skill through play, marked by squeals when one pup bites too hard. The surprising thing? The biting puppy usually looks as startled as the one who got nipped, and this reaction helps them learn appropriate pressure.

TEACHING GENTLE MOUTH SKILLS

When your puppy mouths you during play or petting, allow initial gentle contact. The moment those sharp teeth press too hard, respond with a sharp "ouch" or "stop" and let your hand go completely still. This mimics natural puppy play behavior. Your puppy may pause, surprised by your reaction. Once they relax their mouth, offer calm praise and resume gentle interaction.

If the simple "ouch" technique isn't working, a brief time-out helps. Stop playing for about 30 seconds, then return calmly. For persistent mouthing, walking away briefly shows your puppy that rough play ends the fun. Never hit your puppy or jerk away quickly - these reactions can either escalate the behavior or create fear.

MANAGING EXCITED MOMENTS

Sometimes puppies become overstimulated during play. You might notice a stiffer body, tighter lips, or harder biting. When you spot these signs, calmly end the play session. If holding your puppy, maintain your hold briefly before setting them down. This isn't about punishment - it's about teaching emotional regulation.

THE CHEWING PHASE

Chewing serves multiple purposes for puppies. Beyond exploration, it helps relieve teething discomfort as adult teeth emerge between four and eight months. The process follows a predictable pattern: incisors at 4 months, canines at 5 months, and molars by 6 months. Most puppies complete teething by 8 months, though some may take longer.

Certain breeds, like Labradors and Staffies, have a stronger drive to chew. Intelligence and energy levels also play a role - breeds that need a lot of mental stimulation might chew more when they are bored.

CREATING A CHEW-SAFE ENVIRONMENT

Protect both your puppy and your possessions by removing tempting items like shoes, remote controls, and glasses. Secure electrical cords and remove toxic plants and provide appropriate chew toys, rotating them regularly to maintain interest. Hard rubber toys, specially designed puzzle feeders, and supervised rope toys offer safe options for chewing needs and, as a bonus, they are great fun to watch!

Ready Reference Checklist

Safety Essentials:

- Secure toxic plants and chemicals
- Remove electrical hazards
- Store personal items safely
- Identify emergency vet contact
- Stock appropriate chew toys
- Set up puppy-safe zones

Mouthing behavior might need some professional help if you notice:

- Persistent hard biting
- Signs of aggression
- Regular overstimulation
- Excessive anxiety
- Resistance to gentle training methods

Both mouthing and chewing gradually improve with consistent, patient guidance. Your puppy isn't being naughty - they're learning essential life skills through these natural behaviors.

Puppies not only chew but there is a period when they will use their mouths - a lot! This is called mouthing, and their tiny teeth are remarkably sharp.

They will grab your trouser legs or put their mouth around your hands - and their sharp teeth will take your breath away.

Puppies need to learn about different textures - and human skin is just one of the textures they need to learn about. They also need to understand how hard they can close their jaws, and when enough is enough. They can only learn this by doing it. If you have children then you need to be very aware of this.

4
HOUSE & POTTY TRAINING

One of the main reasons people don't want to have a puppy is the thought of potty training, or specifically, the thought of a dog that is not house-trained and that messes in the home.

House training or potty training your puppy will be one of the first things you do when your puppy comes home. This chapter will guide you through the process, providing tips and exercises to help your puppy learn quickly and effectively.

Materials Needed

- Puppy pads (consider grass-like pads for easier transition)
- Crate
- Cleaning supplies (non-ammonia based)
- Treats
- Leash
- Timer or alarm for scheduled potty breaks

HOW LONG CAN A PUPPY WAIT FOR THE TOILET

The speed at which a puppy learns will vary from puppy to puppy and can often depend on any training that began in his previous home but don't forget that a puppy's bladder grows with them. So when they are younger, it is smaller, which means that they will need to empty it more often.

Generally speaking, a puppy's ability to hold its bladder increases by about an hour per month.

This will mean that at one month, they can hold on for about an hour. By 2 months old, they should be able to hold on for about 2 hours before they need to relieve themselves.

Try not to make them hold on for much more than this over the first few months or there will be accidents. And aim to make sure that your time away from them can tie into their need to go to the toilet.

As a general rule, puppies under 6 months will struggle to hold their bladder for more than 3 or 4 hours, and this should help you work out how long you can be away or when you might need to try and get someone to visit your puppy so that they can relieve themselves outside, rather than in their crate, or in the room they are in.

In terms of pooping, a puppy will poop after food. If you feed your puppy before you leave, make sure that you feed them around 45 minutes before you are due to leave.

This gives you time to take them for a poop. They will normally need to poop between 5 and 30 minutes after a meal.

If you are playing with your puppy before you leave, take them out for a poop after the playtime, as this can also make them want to poop.

Puppy pads should not replace taking your puppy outside often and encouraging him to toilet. Take him out often and praise him every time he toilets.

PUPPY PADS

One of the easiest methods of potty training is to use puppy pads, and some are even made to look like grass. Some breeders also use a litter tray with pine pellets.

I am using puppy pads in this example, but whatever you decide to use you will take the following steps.

Place the puppy pad in the room that he is going to be in. Start doing this the day he comes home. If he looks like he is about to potty, put him on the pad. If he relieves himself, give him lots of praise.

You will soon work out what his behavior is when he needs to toilet so keep an eye on him so that you can react each time. It won't take long - probably around 2-3 days - before he will go to the pad.

Once he is regularly using the pad, start moving it towards the door that you want him to use to go out. Try not to move it too far from where you started the training; just move it slowly to that door.

Once at the door, let him get used to that for a day or two before moving the pad just outside it.

In the final stages, if you notice him starting to toilet in the house, gently pick him up and place him on an 'emergency' pad. Then take him and the pad outside. If there is not enough time to do this, just place him on the pad.

You might want to consider placing the puppy pad at the door that he will be using to access his outside area right away. Of course, this will depend on how far away from the room the household congregates is from that door. You don't want to place it too far from where he will be spending most of his time in these early days.

At every point, every little win, give your puppy lots of praise.

This process can take more time for some puppy's than for others. However, as long as you remember that he will want to relieve himself when he wakes up, after play, and after he eats, then you have a head-start knowing when to expect activity. Make sure you take him outside after each of these events - *don't only rely on the puppy pad.*

It's important never to punish or get angry with your puppy if he toilets in the house. You sometimes see a recommendation to push their face into the mess. Don't do this. It will do the opposite of helping. Getting angry or pushing them may only mean that they don't want to potty in front of you and learn to avoid it as well as making them feel anxious around you.

HOW TO MANAGE POTTY TRAINING

Once your puppy begins the process of going outside to potty, don't forget that every time he relieves himself outdoors, you need to praise him and give him a treat.

Don't do this while he is in the action of potty-time - he will stop to seek the reward, get distracted, and won't finish what he started. It means that he won't be fully relieved when he goes back inside. Instead, wait until he has finished, and don't forget to do this every single time he goes outdoors to potty.

As you do this, use a phrase that he will start to recognize (try not to use 'Good boy' or 'Good girl' - it might cause confusion!).

Instead, use a short phrase such as 'potty' or 'pee pee' or whatever you feel comfortable saying and will remember - just make sure it is one that your pup can begin to recognize with the action he is being asked to complete. They need to know exactly what behavior the reward is for.

This is not only useful when your puppy is young. You will find occasions when you need to encourage your pup to potty (an earlier bedtime, or any schedule change including staying somewhere new). It's good to remember that much of what you teach your puppy now will be of great help throughout your his life. It's also good to think about what phrase you will be stuck with for a long time!

In his early days you will be tempted to take him into the yard every hour to play with him - try not to overdo the this. Stick to around 15 minutes at a time. And don't confuse him by taking him out to play when you want him to potty - the puppy might associate outside as only for play and won't know what is expected of him.

Try and set a clear distinction between when you are taking him out to potty and when you are taking him out to play. The schedule will help plan this and help train you to do both potty and play.

If you live in a flat that has two access doors, then you can use one for play and one for potty!

Where?

Choose a place or a small area outside that you want him to use to relieve himself. As he relieves himself, say your word or specific phrase.

Always take him to the same place every time you take him out to potty - in the morning, the last thing at night, after food, or after play.

If you are using training pads overnight, take the soiled pad to the outside area where you want your puppy to toilet. The scent can help him.

When it is time to take him outside to toilet, avoid playing with him and getting him excited before he relieves himself. Remember, he is easily distracted and will forget what he is there to do.

If your puppy looks a bit confused or doesn't toilet right away, try to encourage him to sniff the ground beside the area you want him to use.

Stay outside until he toilettes. If nothing happens after 5 minutes, don't start to play with him but take his back inside and watch him closely.

After 10 minutes, take him out again and repeat the process until he has done what you need him to do.

THE SIGNS TO WATCH OUT FOR

Try and supervise your puppy at all times when you are trying to potty train him. I know that this is very hard to do, but by supervising and watching him, you will notice how he looks when he starts to feel uncomfortable because his bladder is full, and you will start to recognize how he reacts when this happens.

For example, he might start circling or sniffing the floor, he might be restless, and he may try and go to a place where he has previously done his business.

If you see your puppy mid-toilet, pick him up and take him outside and try to get him to finish what he started; if he does, then gently praise him.

Watch out for any of those signs, or watch out for something your dog does that might signal a change in behavior. Be vigilant; watch, learn, and stay with them if you can.

OVERNIGHT

It is possible that your puppy won't be able to hold his bladder all night long for several months. This means that he will need to relieve himself during the night.

Put some newspaper or puppy pads in his crate. Try and place them in an area that he can avoid. In the morning, don't forget to remove the soiled pad or newspaper and then take it to his outside area to try and draw him to the scent.

If you are going out for any length of time, and you are using his crate, then you will do the same thing. If you can, don't be away for more than 2-3 hours at the start.

It may take several months before your puppy is fully house trained, but the accidents will become less frequent. Try and be patient. It will pay off in time, and in just a few short years, you will have forgotten all about the trials and tribulations of potty training your puppy.

HOW TO CLEAN-UP

It's important to clean the area and try to remove the scent.

Don't use ammonia-based products as this will just encourage them to go to the same place again. Cold water can do the trick too (and it is very good at removing any staining). You can use biological powder, and some people swear by a vinegar-water mix.

As mentioned earlier an enzymatic cleaner (one that uses enzymes which break down and remove organic matter) is a great choice.

YOUR SCHEDULE

One of the best and most effective ways to train your puppy is to get him used to a schedule.

When you first bring your puppy home, make sure that you take him out frequently. Take him out as soon as he wakes up, after playing, and after he has eaten or had a drink.

4-STEP SUMMARY OF A PUPPY SCHEDULE

1. Feed them at the same time and the same frequency, for example, every 2 hours depending on their age
2. Take them out them out as soon as they wake up
3. Take them out before they go to bed
4. Take them out after food and after indoor puppy play.

In terms of how a day might look, try not to forget his sleep time. Your puppy will get sleepy after eating but make sure that you take him out to potty before he goes for his nap.

Once he is older don't feed him right before you take him out for a walk and don't feed him as soon as you return from a walk. The reason you do this is to avoid something called GDV (Gastric Dilatation-Volvulus).

GDV is often known as dog bloat, or a twisted stomach. It is caused by a number of things including large meals, stress, anxiety, excitement and vigorous exercise. It tends to be more common in larger dogs such as German Shepherds but it is worth bearing especially if your pup eats their food extremely fast. This can impact the potential for GDV. If they are very fast easters you can reduce the amount they get fed in one sitting, and compensate by more frequent feeding.

GDV usually occurs within the first two hours of eating, and so the general rule has been to wait 30 minutes after feeding before taking them for a walk and to wait 30 minutes after a walk before feeding them (a gap between exercise and food of 30 minutes). Some vets will recommend waiting for at least two hours after eating before you exercise them and to wait 30 minutes after exercise before feeding.

SLEEP

As mentioned earlier, puppies sleep a lot. When he is young and up to 3 months old, he can sleep 18 hours a day, sometimes up to 20!

He can fall asleep suddenly, and it can even appear as if he has fallen asleep mid-step. He will fall asleep with a chew in his mouth or just sit down in the middle of the floor and collapse. When he does, just pick him up and put him in his crate or basket (with the door open).

He should easily sleep for 7 hours at night, and some puppies can sleep for 7 hours without requiring a bathroom break.

Puppies need their sleep, so make sure you let him get it. This will be harder than you think in the first few weeks. There will be many visitors and lots of people who will want to pick him up and cuddle him. This is okay but don't forget his sleep time. He needs it.

Build this into your schedule so that it might look like this:

7:15 am - wake up and go outside for potty

7:30 am - breakfast

8:00 am - playtime

8:15 am - outside for toilet

8:20 am - sleep (with toy in the cage/depart for work?)

10:15 am - outside for toilet

10:30 - food

10:35 - outside for toilet

11:00 - playtime

11:15 - outside for toilet

11:20 am - sleep with Kong or Toy in the cage

1:15pm - wake up/ outside for toilet

1:20pm - food

1:25 - outside for toilet

2:00 - playtime

2:15 pm - outside for toilet

2:20 - sleep (cage with toy)

And so on. You will find a schedule that works for you as you discover when your puppy likes to go potty during the day. It might be after food or after playtime. But always take him out as soon as he awakens.

The timings will change as he gets a bit older and sleeps less.

STEP-BY-STEP INSTRUCTIONS

Understanding Puppy Bladder Capacity

A puppy's ability to hold its bladder increases by about an hour per month.

At one month, they can hold on for about an hour. At two months, about two hours, and so on.

Puppies under six months will struggle to hold their bladder for more than 3-4 hours.

Establishing a Potty Routine

- Take your puppy out as soon as they wake up, after eating, after playing, and before bedtime.
- Choose a specific spot outside for your puppy to relieve themselves and use a consistent phrase like "go potty" or "do your business."
- Keep a consistent schedule to help your puppy learn when and where to go.

Using Puppy Pads

- Place puppy pads in a designated area inside your home.
- Gradually move the pads closer to the door and eventually outside.
- Praise your puppy when they use the pads correctly.

Dealing with Accidents

- Accidents will happen; it's part of the learning process.
- Clean the area thoroughly to remove any scent using non-ammonia-based cleaners.
- Do not punish your puppy for accidents as this can lead to fear and confusion.

INTERACTIVE CHECKLIST

Before starting house training:

- Establish a consistent routine
- Choose a designated potty spot
- Purchase puppy pads and a crate (see the next chapter)

During training:

- Take your puppy out frequently
- Use a consistent phrase for potty time
- Praise and reward your puppy for successful potty trips

Don't forget to use a body signal - for example move your arm from the centre of your body and aim it toward the door before you take him out, when you ask him to potty you might flatten your hand and lower it in front of your stomach.

Fill-in-the-Blank

My puppy's designated potty spot:

_____

The signal I will use as I go the the door is:

_____

The signal I will use once we are outside to encourage him to potty is:

_____

The phrase I will use for potty time:

_____

My puppy's usual potty times (after waking up, after eating, etc.):

_____

_____

_____

_____

PRACTICE EXERCISES

Routine Establishment Exercise

Create a schedule for taking your puppy out to potty.

Date:

Times for potty breaks:

Observation Exercise:

Spend 10 minutes observing your puppy and note their body language and behavior.

Date:

Behaviors observed:

_____

_____

_____

_____

_____

Praise and Reward Exercise

Practice praising and rewarding your puppy immediately after they potty outside. Ideally, you want to rate each treat - you are trying to discover a ranking of his most favorite to his, still enjoyable, least favorite (usually kibble).

Date:

Type of reward used: _____

Puppy's reaction

_____

_____

REAL-LIFE SCENARIOS

Scenario: First Night at Home

Your puppy needs to go potty during the night. Record your actions and the outcome.

Steps taken:

_____

_____

Did your puppy successfully potty outside? (Yes/No) _____

Notes:

_____

_____

Scenario: Introducing Puppy Pads

Start using puppy pads and gradually move them towards the door.

Date started: _____

Did your puppy use the pads correctly? (Yes/No) ___

Progress notes:

_____

_____

. . .

Scenario: Dealing with an Accident

Your puppy has an accident in the house. Record how you handled it.

Date:

Puppy's reaction:

Cleaning method used:

_____

_____

Scenario: Leaving Your Puppy Alone

Plan for times when you need to leave your puppy alone. Record how they managed. Include date, duration of time left alone, note whether there were any accidents and add any other relevant notes.

Date:

Duration of time left alone:

Any accidents? (Yes/No) _____

Notes:

_____

_____

Fill-in-the-Blank Schedule

Morning routine:

_____

Afternoon routine:

Evening routine:

Bedtime routine:

Remember, the occasional accident is part of the process, and soon, you'll have a well-trained companion. Use the tracker on the following pages to train yourself as well as your puppy!

Tracking Progress

Date	Potty Break Times	Successful Potty Trips	Notes

5

CRATE TRAINING

The goal of crate training is to create a space where your puppy feels secure and comfortable, viewing the crate as their own "den." This chapter will guide you through the essentials of crate training, the benefits, and step-by-step exercises to help your puppy adjust.

Additionally, tracking exercises and a progress log are included to ensure you know when your puppy is progressing and to provide cause for celebration!

Ensure the crate is comfortable and associate it with positive experiences. You can do this by giving him a kong filled with treats or food that he loves (liver cake, or something soft that he can work on) Never use the crate as a form of punishment.

WHY CRATE TRAINING IS IMPORTANT

Crate training is a valuable tool for both you and your puppy. Here are the primary benefits:

• **House Training:** Dogs don't like to soil their sleeping area, so the crate helps your puppy learn to control their bladder and bowels.

• **Safe Space:** The crate becomes your puppy's personal sanctuary, providing a retreat where they feel safe and secure.

• **Travel and Safety:** The crate can be used when traveling or staying in unfamiliar places, reducing anxiety for your dog. It also ensures their safety when left alone at home or in the car.

• **Chew Prevention:** Puppies often chew due to teething or boredom. Crating them while unsupervised prevents them from damaging furniture or other items.

MATERIALS NEEDED

• **Crate:** Choose the right size and type (plastic, wire, or fabric).

• **Blanket or bedding:** Soft and comfortable, preferably with a familiar scent.

• **Toys:** Provide chew toys and a Kong filled with treats to keep your puppy occupied.

• **Treats:** High-value treats for rewarding good behavior in the crate.

• **Optional:** Crate cover (to make the crate feel more den-like), especially at night.

STEP-BY-STEP INSTRUCTIONS

1. Introducing Your Puppy to the Crate

Step 1: Before your puppy comes home, set up the crate with a soft blanket or bedding. If possible, include an item with a familiar scent (like a towel or blanket from their breeder or previous home).

Step 2: Place the crate in a room where the family spends time. This allows the puppy to explore the crate without feeling isolated.

Step 3: Encourage curiosity by placing treats around and near the crate. Allow your puppy to explore the area without pressure.

Step 4: Gradually move the treats closer to the door and then inside the crate, praising them for any curiosity or steps taken toward entering.

2. Getting Comfortable Inside the Crate

Step 1: Once your puppy is comfortable around the crate, start feeding them near the crate. Place their food bowl beside the crate door, and slowly move it inside over time.

Step 2: When they start entering the crate for food or toys, don't close the door initially. Let them explore freely, entering and exiting the crate at their own pace.

Step 3: Gradually extend the time your puppy spends inside the crate by feeding meals or giving them a Kong toy with treats. Close the door only once they are comfortable staying in the crate.

3. Closing the Crate Door

Step 1: When your puppy is happy to stay in the crate, close the door for short periods (1-2 minutes) while they're occupied with a toy or treat.

Step 2: Gradually increase the time the door is closed, up to 10 minutes. Open the door calmly if they show no signs of distress.

Step 3: If your puppy becomes anxious (whining, barking, or panting), go back to shorter intervals and increase the time more gradually.

4. Leaving the Room

Step 1: Once your puppy is comfortable with the crate door closed for up to 10 minutes, start leaving the room for short periods. Begin with just a minute or two and increase the time gradually.

Step 2: If your puppy whines or barks, do not return immediately. Wait for a pause before entering the room to avoid reinforcing negative behavior.

Step 3: Aim to have your puppy stay in the crate for 30 minutes while you are out of sight before moving on to leaving the house.

5. Nighttime Crate Training

Step 1: In the early days, place the crate in your bedroom at night. This helps the puppy feel secure as they adjust to their new home.

Step 2: After a few days, move the crate to the designated sleeping area. Turn out the lights or leave a low-level light to signal that it's sleep time.

Step 3: Take your puppy out to toilet during the night if needed, but do so without much fuss to avoid overstimulation.

INTERACTIVE CHECKLIST

Before Starting Crate Training:

- Have you chosen the right size crate?
- Is there comfortable bedding in the crate?
- Have you placed toys and familiar-scented items in the crate?

After Each Training Session:

Did your puppy explore the crate voluntarily? (Yes/No)

Did they stay calm inside the crate? (Yes/No)

How many minutes did they stay in the crate without distress?

Did you reward your puppy for entering the crate? (Yes/No)

You can use the following tables as a guide and add anything else that you would like to track. For example, if you are starting the overnight training in your bedroom then mark the location and its success, The tables at the end of the chapter are only examples but they might help you think about the different phases and what to watch out for. Of you are reading on kindle then use the prompts and note down your answers.

CRATE TRAINING EXERCISES

Exploring the Crate

Let your puppy explore the crate without pressure.

Use treats and toys to make the crate a fun and rewarding place.

Record your observations:

Date: _____

Did your puppy enter the crate voluntarily? (Yes/No)

Any signs of stress? (Yes/No) If yes, describe:

_____

Crate with Door Closed

Once your puppy is comfortable inside, close the crate door for short periods and gradually extend the time the door is closed.

Record progress

Date: _____

Time spent with the door closed: _____

Success rate: _____

Any signs of distress? (Yes/No) If yes, describe:

_____

_____

TROUBLESHOOTING

If Your Puppy Won't Enter the Crate

Use high-value treats or favorite toys to lure them inside.

Be patient and take it slow. Don't rush the process.

If Your Puppy Whines or Barks

Don't open the door immediately. Wait for a moment of quiet before letting them out.

Gradually increase crate time to avoid overwhelming your puppy.

If Your Puppy Refuses to Stay in the Crate

Go back to shorter crate times and work on building positive associations with the crate using toys and treats.

CRATE TRAINING TIPS

Use Positive Reinforcement: Always reward your puppy for good behavior inside the crate.

Gradual Progress: Build up crate time slowly to ensure your puppy is comfortable.

No Punishment: Never use the crate as a form of punishment. It should always be a positive space for your puppy.

Consistency: Use the crate regularly to help your puppy feel safe and secure.

Exercise: Make sure your puppy gets plenty of exercise before crate time to help them settle down.

SCENARIOS

Crate Training Beginner Exercise

Introduce your puppy to the crate, making it a positive space with toys and treats.

Date: _____

Puppy's reaction to crate:

_____

Out of Sight Training

Practice leaving the room while your puppy is in the crate.

Start with just a few minutes and gradually increase the time.

Record progress:

Date: _____

Time spent out of sight: _____

Success rate: _____

Any signs of anxiety? (Yes/No)

If yes, describe:

_____

_____

Scenario: Crate Training Overnight

Practice using the crate overnight with your puppy sleeping inside.

Record the outcome:

Did your puppy sleep through the night? (Yes/No)

Any middle-of-the-night wake-ups? (Yes/No).

If yes, describe:

_____

_____

Scenario: Crate Training During Travel

Take the crate along for a short trip in the car or during a visit to a friend's house. Observe how your puppy reacts to the crate in a new environment.

Record the outcome

Was your puppy comfortable in the crate? (Yes/No)

Did they settle down quickly? (Yes/No)

Notes:

_____

_____

Use the tables on the following pages as a basis for you and your puppy's progress tracking.

Tracking Progress: Exploring The Crate

Date	Time in Crate	Attempts	Success/Fail	Success Rate (%)I	Notes
	3 mins	4	1	25%	Toy and rug was placed isnide - went in and out without much interest other thatn sniffing
	3 mins	4	3	75%	Played with the Kong that had hotdog inside

Tracking Progress: Crate With Door Closed

Date	Time in Crate	Attempts	Success/Fail	Success Rate (%)|	Notes
	3 mins	4	1	25%	Played with the Kong that had hotdog inside but ran to door when closed (we were in sight)
	5 mins	4	3	75%	Played with the Kong that had cheese inside and bed placed at end (we were in sight)

Tracking Progress: Crate With Me/Family Out of Sight

Date	Time in Crate	Attempts	Success/Fail	Success Rate (%)	Notes
	3 mins	4	1	25%	Played with the Kong that had cheese inside and bed placed at end (we were in sight)
	5 mins	4	3	75%	Played with the Kong that had cheese inside and bed placed at end (we were in sight). Toys added. We returned as soon as heard bark then extended a minute at a time.

Tracking Progress: Overnight

Date	Time in Crate	Attempts	Success/Fail	Success Rate (%)	Notes
	60 mins	4	1	25%	Played with the Kong that had cheese inside and bed placed at end.. Toys added and followed same routine as we did with the door closed when we were out of sight. Left room for 60 minutes.
	60 mins	4	3	75%	Fell asleep and didn't wake up when we went back - looked tired.

6

BASIC CUES: SIT

Teach your puppy the essential commands of "sit," "stay," and "release" to ensure they are well-behaved and responsive. These foundational behaviors are crucial for safety and effective communication with your pup and you can begin saying the words before he can go out for a walk and within the first few days after your pup gets home.

TEACHING YOUR PUPPY TO SIT

Materials Needed:

- Small, high-value treats (soft and easy to chew)
- Clicker (optional, for clicker training)
- Quiet, distraction-free area for initial training

STEP-BY-STEP INSTRUCTIONS

1 Get Your Puppy's Attention

- Call your puppy's name to ensure they are focused on you.
- Hold a treat in your hand to grab their interest.

2 Lure Your Puppy into a Sit

- Hold the treat close to your puppy's nose.
- Slowly move the treat upwards and backwards over their head. As their nose follows the treat, their bottom should naturally lower to the ground.

3 Mark the Behavior

- The moment your puppy's bottom touches the ground, say "Sit" and immediately give them the treat.
- If you're using a clicker, click as soon as they sit, then give the treat.

4 Practice and Repeat

- Repeat the process several times in short training sessions (5-10 minutes).
- Practice in different locations and with varying levels of distractions as your puppy gets better.

TRAINING TIPS

Use a Clear, Consistent Command: Always use the same word, "Sit," and say it in a calm, clear voice. Introduce a hand signal. Bend your arm at the elbow, with your palm facing you and lift your arm up towards your face.

Positive Reinforcement: Reward your puppy immediately when they sit to reinforce the behavior.

Patience and Consistency: Training takes time. Be patient and consistent with your commands and rewards.

INTERACTIVE CHECKLIST

Before you start:

- Choose a quiet area for training
- Have a bag of high-value treats ready
- Optional: Have a clicker for clicker training

After the session:

- Did your puppy sit successfully? (Yes/No)
- Did you reward your puppy immediately? (Yes/No)
- How many successful sits did your puppy achieve?

TROUBLESHOOTING

If Your Puppy Doesn't Sit:

- Ensure you are holding the treat correctly and moving it slowly enough for them to follow. Remember you are trying to get them to have no option but to sit as you move treat slightly above their nose, moving it backwards
- Practice in a quieter area with fewer distractions.

If Your Puppy Jumps for the Treat:

- Hold the treat closer to their nose and move it more slowly.
- Lower the treat slightly to keep them from jumping up.

PRACTICE EXERCISES

1. Repetition Drills:

Perform 5-10 repetitions of the sit command in a single session.

Gradually increase the number of repetitions as your puppy becomes more comfortable.

2. Record your progress:

Date: _____

Number of repetitions: _____

Successful sits: _____

Notes:

_____

3. Generalization:

Practice the "Sit" command in different rooms and outdoor environments to help your puppy generalize the behavior.

Use different types of treats to maintain interest.

4. Record your observations:

Environment (e.g., living room, backyard):

_____

Success rate: _____

Any distractions? (Yes/No) If yes, describe:

_____

5. Duration and Distractions:

Once your puppy consistently sits on command, start increasing the duration they stay sitting before giving the treat. Introduce mild distractions and practice until they can sit reliably despite the distractions.

6. Record progress:

Duration before treat: _____

Types of distractions introduced: _____

Success rate: _____

Notes:_____

REAL-LIFE SCENARIOS

Scenario 1: You're in the park, and another dog walks by. Practice the sit command with your puppy. Record how they responded:

Was your puppy able to sit? (Yes/No)

Did they stay seated despite the distraction? (Yes/No)

Notes:

_____

Scenario 2: A guest arrives at your home. Use the sit command to manage your puppy's excitement. Record the outcome:

Was your puppy able to sit when the guest arrived? (Yes/No)

How long did they stay seated? _____

Notes:

_____

7

BASIC CUES: STAY

Objective:

Teach your puppy the "stay" command to ensure they remain in place until given a release cue, improving their self-control and safety.

Materials Needed:

1. Small, high-value treats (soft and easy to chew)
2. Clicker (optional, for clicker training)
3. Quiet, distraction-free area for initial training

STEP-BY-STEP INSTRUCTIONS

Get Your Puppy's Attention

Call your puppy's name to ensure they are focused on you.

Hold a treat in your hand to grab their interest.

Introduce the Stay Command

Step 1: Ask your puppy to sit.

Step 2: Hold your hand out with your palm facing them and say "stay."

Step 3: Take a step back while maintaining eye contact.

Step 4: After a brief moment, step back to your puppy and reward them with a treat if they stayed in place.

Increase Distance and Duration

Step 1: Gradually increase the distance by taking more steps back.

Step 2: Gradually increase the duration by waiting longer before returning to your puppy.

Step 3: Always return to your puppy to reward them for staying in place, reinforcing the stay behavior.

Add Distractions Gradually

Step 1: Introduce mild distractions, such as another person walking by or a toy placed nearby.

Step 2: Gradually increase the level of distractions as your puppy becomes more proficient at staying.

Step 3: Reward your puppy generously for staying despite the distractions.

Proofing the Stay Command

Step 1: Practice in various environments to generalize the behavior.

Step 2: Start with low-distraction areas and progressively move to more challenging environments.

Step 3: Ensure your puppy succeeds by gradually increasing the difficulty and always rewarding them for staying.

Step 4: Of you haven't already done so, introduce you hand signal.

Troubleshooting

Step 1: If your puppy breaks the stay, calmly return them to the original position and try again.

Step 2: Shorten the distance and duration if they are struggling, then gradually increase again.

Step 3: Maintain a calm and positive demeanor to avoid frustrating your puppy.

TRAINING TIPS

Use a Clear, Consistent Command: Always use the same word, "Stay," and say it in a calm, clear voice.

Positive Reinforcement: Reward your puppy immediately when they stay to reinforce the behavior.

Patience and Consistency: Training takes time. Be patient and consistent with your commands and rewards.

INTERACTIVE CHECKLIST

Before starting stay training:

- Choose a quiet area for training
- Have a bag of high-value treats ready
- Optional: Have a clicker for clicker training

After the session:

- Did your puppy stay successfully? (Yes/No)
- Did you reward your puppy immediately? (Yes/No)
- How many successful stays did your puppy achieve? _____

TROUBLESHOOTING

If Your Puppy Doesn't Stay:

Ensure you are holding the treat correctly and moving away slowly enough for them to follow.

Practice in a quieter area with fewer distractions.

If Your Puppy Breaks the Stay:

Calmly return them to the original position and shorten the distance Maintain a calm demeanor and try again.

PRACTICE EXERCISES

Repetition Drills:

Perform 5-10 repetitions of the stay command in a single session.

Gradually increase the number of repetitions as your puppy becomes more comfortable.

Record your progress:

Date: _____

Number of repetitions: _____

Notes:

_____

_____

Generalization

Practice the "Stay" command in different rooms and outdoor environments to help your puppy generalize the behavior.

Use different types of treats to maintain interest.

Record your observations:

Environment (e.g., living room, backyard): _____

Success rate: _____

Any distractions? (Yes/No) If yes, describe:

_____

Duration and Distractions

Once your puppy consistently stays on command, start increasing the duration they stay before giving the treat.

Introduce mild distractions and practice until they can stay reliably despite the distractions.

Record progress:

Duration before treat: _____

Types of distractions introduced: _____

Success rate: _____

REAL-LIFE SCENARIOS

Scenario: Stay at the Door

Steps:

Ask your puppy to stay when someone knocks at the door.

Reward your puppy for staying despite the distraction.

Record:

Date: _____

Puppy's response:

_____

Scenario: Stay in Public

Steps:

Ask your puppy to stay during a walk in a busy area.

Reward your puppy for staying despite the distractions.

Record:

Date: _____
Puppy's response:

_____

Distraction Sensitivity Chart

Use the following table as a guide and create your own table to track distraction levels and work out what your puppy reacts to.

Tracking Progress: Stay Cue and Distraction Example

Date	Distraction Level	Type of Distraction	Puppies Response	Notes
	Low	Family members sitting	Released and responded	
	Low	Soft background music	Released and responded	
	Medium	Family members moving	Needed extra encouragement	
	Medium	Doorbell ringing	Released after second cue	
	High	Other dogs playing nearby	Needed multiple cues	
	High	Children running	Released with difficulty	
	High	Squirrels in the vicinity	Needed re-cue	

Tracking Progress: Stay Cue and Distraction

Date	Distraction Level	Type of Distraction	Puppies Response	Notes

Tracking Progress: Stay Cue and Distraction

Date	Distraction Level	Type of Distraction	Puppies Response	Notes

8

BASIC CUES: RELEASE

The release cue is crucial because it provides a clear signal to your puppy that they are free to move from the stay position. This helps prevent confusion and ensures that your puppy knows exactly when they are expected to stay and when they can move. A well-taught release cue also reinforces the importance of waiting patiently until given permission to move, which is essential for their safety and self-control.

Examples of Release Commands

Okay: Commonly used and easy to remember.

Go: Simple and direct.

Free: Indicates that the puppy is no longer under command.

Release: Explicitly states the purpose of the cue.

Break: Signifies the end of the command.

Use Consistent Cues:

- Always use the same verbal and visual cues for sit, stay, and release.
- Consistency helps your puppy understand and respond correctly.

Gradual Progression:

- Gradually increase the duration of the stay before the release cue.
- Ensure each step is mastered before moving to the next.

Positive Reinforcement:

- Always reward your puppy for successful stays and releases.
- Use high-value treats and praise to motivate your puppy.

Practice in Different Environments

Practice the sit stay release sequence in various environments to generalize the behavior.

Start with low-distraction areas and move to more challenging environments.

TRAINING OBJECTIVE

Teach your puppy the "release" command to signal the end of a stay, ensuring they know when they are free to move.

Materials Needed:

- Small, high-value treats (soft and easy to chew)
- Clicker (optional, for clicker training)
- Quiet, distraction-free area for initial training

STEP-BY-STEP INSTRUCTIONS

Get Your Puppy's Attention

- Call your puppy's name to ensure they are focused on you.
- Hold a treat in your hand to grab their interest.

Introduce the Release Cue

Step 1: Ask your puppy to sit and stay.

Step 2: After a short duration, say your chosen release cue ("okay" or "go") in an excited tone.

Step 3: Encourage your puppy to move from their position and reward them.

Practicing the Sequence

Step 1: Practice the sequence: sit, stay, release.

Step 2: Gradually increase the duration of the stay before giving the release cue.

Step 3: Always use the release cue to signal the end of the stay, ensuring your puppy learns the meaning of the cue.

Reinforcing with Positive Experiences

Step 1: Ensure that the release is associated with positive experiences, like playtime or treats.

Step 2: Gradually increase the time between the stay and the release cue to build your puppy's patience.

Generalizing the Release Cue

Step 1: Practice the release cue in different environments and with various distractions.

Step 2: Ensure consistency in using the release cue to help your puppy generalize the behavior across different contexts.

Troubleshooting

Step 1: If your puppy doesn't move on the release cue, use a more excited tone or gently encourage them with a treat.

Step 2: If your puppy anticipates the release, reinforce the stay until the release cue is given.

TRAINING TIPS

Use a Clear, Consistent Command: Always use the same word, "Release," and say it in a calm, clear voice.

Positive Reinforcement: Reward your puppy immediately when they respond to the release cue.

Patience and Consistency: Training takes time. Be patient and consistent with your commands and rewards.

INTERACTIVE CHECKLIST

Before starting release training:

- Choose a quiet area for training
- Have a bag of high-value treats ready
- Optional: Have a clicker for clicker training

After the session:

Did your puppy release successfully? (Yes/No) _____

Did you reward your puppy immediately? (Yes/No) _____

How many successful releases did your puppy achieve? _____

TROUBLESHOOTING

If Your Puppy Doesn't Release:

Ensure you are using an excited tone and possibly a gentle physical cue.

Practice in a quieter area with fewer distractions.

If Your Puppy Anticipates the Release:

Reinforce the stay until the release cue is given.

Be consistent and patient to ensure they wait for the release command.

PRACTICE EXERCISES

Repetition Drills:

Perform 5-10 repetitions of the release command in a single session.

Gradually increase the number of repetitions as your puppy becomes more comfortable.

Record your progress:

Date: _____

Number of repetitions: _____

Successful releases: _____

Notes:

_____

_____

GENERALIZATION

Practice the "Release" command in different rooms and outdoor Use different types of treats to maintain interest.

Record your observations:

Environment (e.g., living room, backyard): _____

Success rate: _____

Any distractions? (Yes/No) If yes, describe: _____

DURATION AND DISTRACTIONS

Once your puppy consistently releases on command, start increasing the duration they stay before giving the release cue.

Introduce mild distractions and practice until they can release reliably despite the distractions.

Record progress:

Duration before release: _____

Types of distractions introduced: _____

Success rate: _____

Use the table at the end of this chapter as an example of how to track progress and identify what needs more work (and why).

REAL-LIFE SCENARIOS

Scenario: Release at the Door

Steps:

Ask your puppy to stay when someone knocks at the door.

Use the release cue after a short stay and reward your puppy for responding.

Record:

Date: _____

Puppy's response: _____

Scenario: Release in Public

Steps:

Ask your puppy to stay during a walk in a busy area.

Use the release cue and reward your puppy for responding despite the distractions.

Record:

Date: _____

Puppy's response: _____

9
SUMMARY AND EXERCISES OF THE BASIC CUE'S

FILL-IN-THE-BLANK

My puppy's sit cue: _____

My puppy's stay cue: _____

My puppy's release cue: _____

SIT-STAY-RELEASE EXERCISES

Basic Sit Exercise

Practice the sit command in a low-distraction environment.

Date: _____

Success rate: _____

Basic Stay Exercise

Practice the stay command with short distances and durations.

Date: _____

Distance: _____

Duration: _____

Basic Release Exercise

Practice the release command after a short stay.

Date: _____

Release cue used: _____

Success rate: _____

Intermediate Stay Exercise

Increase the distance and duration of the stay command.

Date: _____

Distance: _____

Duration: _____

Advanced Sit Stay Release Exercise

Practice the sit, stay, release sequence in a high-distraction environment.

Date: _____

Environment: _____

Success rate: _____

. . .

Sit Stay at the Door

Steps:

Practice sit stay when someone knocks at the door.

Reward your puppy for staying despite the distraction.

Record:

Date: _____

Puppy's response: _____

Sit Stay in Public

Steps:

Practice sit stay during a walk in a busy area.

Reward your puppy for staying despite the distractions.

Record:

Date: _____

Puppy's response: _____

Sit Stay Release in the Park

Steps:

Practice the sit stay release sequence at a park with distractions.

Reward your puppy for following the commands despite the distractions.

Record:

Date: _____

Puppy's response: _____

DISTRACTION EXAMPLES

Low-Level Distractions

• Family members sitting quietly

• Soft background music

• Toys scattered around

Medium-Level Distractions:

• Family members moving around

• Doorbell ringing

• Television on

High-Level Distractions:

• Other dogs playing nearby

• Children running and shouting

• Squirrels or birds in the vicinity

ADDITIONAL TIPS

Use Consistent Cues:

Always use the same verbal and visual cues for sit, stay, and release.

Consistency helps your puppy understand and respond correctly.

Gradual Progression:

Gradually increase the difficulty of the stay by adding distance, duration, and distractions.

Ensure each step is mastered before moving to the next.

Positive Reinforcement:

Always reward your puppy for successful sits, stays, and releases.

Use high-value treats and praise to motivate your puppy.

Practice in Different Environments:

Practice the sit stay release sequence in various environments to generalize the behavior.

Start with low-distraction areas and move to more challenging environments.

Tracking Progress: Release Cue and Distraction

Date	Attempt Number	Duration of Stay (seconds)	Distraction Level	Release Cue Used	Cue Success (Yes/No)	Success Rate (%)	What Went Well	Needs Improvement
	1	Family members sitting	Low	Okay	Yes	10%	Puppy stayed calm and followed the cue.	Increase distraction level gradually
	2	10	Medium	Go	No	50%	Puppy initially stayed but broke due to movement.	Practice with moving distractions more often
	3	15	High	Release	Yes	75%	Puppy responded to the release cue quickly.	Work on consistency with high distractions

10

LEASH, RECALL AND THE HEAL POSITION

Teaching your puppy to walk nicely on a leash and come when called forms the foundation of your lifelong relationship. These skills create safety, build trust, and allow your puppy to enjoy greater freedom. Before diving into specific training, let's understand what makes these skills so essential.

Your puppy needs to recognize and respond to their name, maintain focus on you, and understand basic commands like 'sit' before advancing to leash and recall work. These building blocks create the communication channel necessary for more complex training.

MASTERING THE LEASH

The way you handle the leash directly affects how your puppy learns to walk beside you.

Hold the leash end in your right hand, allowing it to cross naturally in front of your body. Your left hand becomes the control point, positioned palm-down closer to your puppy. Keep treats readily accessible in your right hand – you'll need them frequently during early training.

Start with your puppy in a sitting position beside your left leg. Choose a consistent phrase like 'let's go' to signal the beginning of movement. As you start walking, use your left hand to guide while holding a treat at nose level exactly where you want your puppy positioned. This creates a natural incentive to stay in the correct spot.

When you need to change direction, use clear, consistent cues. 'This way' works well, but avoid words you might need for other commands. Your puppy will quickly learn that this phrase signals a change in direction.

The secret to loose-leash walking lies in patience and timing. When your puppy creates tension in the leash, simply stop. Don't pull back – just wait. The moment your puppy moves back toward you, creating slack in the leash, mark this behavior with praise or a clicker and reward. This teaches your puppy that walking beside you brings rewards, while pulling stops all forward progress.

THE ART OF RECALL

Dogs train better when they are making their own choices. You are aiming to have your dog return to you on cue no matter how many other exciting things are going on around him. This means that your puppy needs to want to return to you on cue, not only when there are no other dogs around, but also when there are dogs to play with.

You can only achieve this if you are more interesting than whatever else he is doing, and if he is listening and paying attention to you.

In summary, you want him to stop what he is doing; you want him to look at you, and you want him to walk beside you, or come to you on cue.

Begin this vital training indoors where distractions are minimal. Choose your recall word – most handlers use 'come' or 'here' – and stick with it absolutely. Pair your verbal cue with a consistent hand signal; opening your arms welcomingly works well and creates an inviting gesture your puppy can see from a distance.

Start recall training by making yourself irresistible. Call your puppy for meals, before play sessions, and during quiet moments. Keep these early sessions brief, under ten minutes, and always reward generously when your puppy responds. Every successful recall builds the foundation for future reliability.

As your puppy masters indoor recalls, move to garden practice using a long training line. This special leash provides safety while allowing your puppy more freedom to explore. Hold the line's end in your right hand, controlling the slack through your left. Allow natural movement but maintain the ability to guide gently when needed. Never jerk or pull harshly – the line exists for safety, not correction.

TRAINING OUTSIDE

Training for recall outside of the house begins in the garden or any other enclosed space. It is here that he is going to find the most distractions.

This is when you are going to work with the clicker and training leads and when you will start working out the value that he attaches to each of his different treats if you haven't already done so.

A great tip is to train your puppy before he has eaten - this means the treat you are offering will be of higher value to him and he will be more interested in them! And don't train him for too long. Pay attention if he looks like he is getting bored and stop the training and start again the next day.

To get started, put your puppy in his harness and on his training leash. Just like the early indoor training, you can start with rewarding an action with no other cues, to get him used to the long-line and outdoor training. He will know what to do quickly, because he has already been trained indoors.

The difference now is that you are going to place something he might want to eat or might want to get (a toy), a short distance away from him, and within the length of the leash, or just a bit further away. You are now introducing something he wants to get to but that is away from you.

As he goes towards the object or the treat (but not too tasty), tighten his leash and say his name then the cue e.g. 'Barney 'come'. As soon as he turns and comes (even if it's only a step or two) reward and praise him.

If you are using a clicker, you will click as soon as he turns. Aim to have an even tastier treat for him than the one he was going towards. You want to increase the value of the treats the more you want him to do something, so that he prefers to choose that tastier treat.

By having the leash on him, you can also gently encourage him to come towards you to get his reward if you need to. The leash helps you have a bit of control over this recall in the early stages as he continues to establish the cue 'come' outside of the house, and where he will want to explore more.

You will also play on the training leash and long line. Give him a few treats then run forward or backward a few steps and say 'Barney, Come!' in a playful voice while holding a treat out at the height of his nose (so that all of his feet are on the ground) and as he reaches you give him the treat.

You can extend this game to add the sit. As he reaches you to get his treat, move the treat up in front of his nose, so that he is forced back into the sit position to get his treat. In this way the come and sit are the same cue which means when you ask him to come, he will come to you and sit without being asked to sit.

You can, and should start practicing this as soon as you can. Puppies learn most up to the age of 18 weeks.

The next step for recall training is to have him move further away from you, and for him to return when he hears his cue. Good recall means he does this all the time. If he is not, then he is not ready, and you won't want to risk letting him off-leash. You will have already trained him to come and you are now continuing to establish this outside of the home.

To understand what you are asking your puppy to do, think about it like this. He is exploring and having fun, he is finding interesting and exciting things to sniff and play with. When you call him, you want him to prefer to come to you rather than keep doing whatever he is enjoying. If you can achieve this, then there is no reason for him not to return to you when called.

To do this you will want to start including training games and you will have worked out what his favorite treats are, and which ones top the list - it could be cheese, hotdogs, carrots, and lastly kibble.

BUILDING DISTANCE AND RELIABILITY

As your puppy's skills improve, gradually increase the challenge. Add distance in safe, enclosed areas. Introduce mild distractions one at a time. Practice recalls during play, during meals, and during exciting moments. Your puppy needs to learn that responding to your call brings rewards better than any distraction.

Remember that successful returns deserve celebration, no matter how long they take. Never punish a delayed return – doing so teaches your puppy that coming to you brings unpleasant consequences. Instead, focus on making every recall a joyful reunion.

Like most training sessions, keep the training to around 10 minutes and watch out for any signs that he is getting stressed (quick head movements, grabbing the treat/food, ears flat) and try not to get him over-excited.

If your puppy is a part of a household then get all members involved in the training too. Don't forget to ask him to do something you know he can do at the end of the training so that it ends in success. You want him to enjoy his training.

You won't let him off leash outside in an unenclosed area until you are happy that he will return to you.

To do this you need to introduce him to different locations and train him in these locations - different rooms in the house, different areas of the garden or different areas of an enclosed area. You will then introduce lots of distractions as the training develops - a toy, another person, another dog that you know (and that you know is vaccinated) etc and you will keep doing the training exercises with all these distractions present.

You are aiming to get him to always pay attention to you and to always return to you despite any exciting activity or scents that he might be interested in - and if he can get used to this in a safe garden then he will be familiar with what to do once he gets to the park.

When it comes to recall, you should wait until his recall is up to about 70%-80% before you start adding the distraction element of his recall training.

RANDOM AND VARIABLE REINFORCEMENT

The best way to train your puppy is using random and variable reinforcement. All this means is that over time change how often he gets a treat for the same behavior, so that he is hoping for it each time (don't wait too long to reward as you start to reduce the level of treats) and change the value of the treat (for a really good response).

If you want to, you can measure the average response time for recall (either daily or per 12 returns, etc.) so that when he comes back faster, he gets a super tasty treat. This is the most effective way to train your puppy to become addicted to coming back to you.

One last trick - if your puppy has taken a while to return on cue then, when he arrives, show him the treat and put it back in your pocket. As he moves away ask him to 'come' and, when he gets to you, give him his treat. This will help him learn that acting right away gets the reward.

USING THE LONG-LINE

You don't need to use the long-line but it can be really helpful and, if you can, I would recommend it. To describe how this is done I picked a hand but you will end up doing something that works for you.

Practice this in a garden if you can, and, in the beginning, have no other distractions. You want to get used to working with the long line and you also want to test that your training is working.

Hold the end of the line in your right hand so that you have it tightly held. Wrap the length of the line into loops so that you can slowly release the line over the front of your body, feeding it through your left hand, making sure it can be easily released.

In your left hand, you are holding the part of the line that is acting as your dog leash, and it is attached to his harness, and your hand is operating as a feeder, controlling the delivery of the line.

This means you can slowly release the line through your left hand, to allow your puppy to move away from you, or clamp it closed (gently) to slow or stop the release of the line.

You will have your right hand holding the end of the long line as well as the loops of the spare line. Once you are comfortable you can start the training.

Slowly move in a circle on the same spot so that he is running around you, loosening the line so that he can move away from you, and then call him back to you. Just get him used to the leash and watching you, and knowing that he gets a reward when he comes back.

You can then add a game (and later you can play this off-leash too), by throwing a treat away from you, and letting your puppy go towards the treat.

Once he has eaten his treat, call his name to get his attention, wait until he looks at you (click), 'come' (cue), and when he comes to you (praise/reward). Then throw another treat in a different direction so that he is constantly running away and towards you in a fun game.

When you need to tighten or 'pull' the line to encourage him to come back on his cue, move or lean forward rather than move against him, and gently make the line shorter. This allows you to be in control of your puppy whilst letting him return without feeling 'pulled'.

The final part is to wait until he is preoccupied with something and is not looking at you. Get his attention and ask him to come. If he comes then praise and reward. If he doesn't come, just walk to him and show him all the treats you have, and then walk away from him.

He is likely to follow you to try and get a treat. Just ignore him. As soon as he isn't right beside you, ask him to come to you. When he does, give him lots of praise and a favorite treat. It won't take long for him to realise that coming is much better than not coming.

The next step is to repeat the indoor sit stay come training in the outdoor environment. Just as you did indoors get your puppy to sit-stay and then move away from him while still facing him and then ask him to 'come'. e.g., 'Barney, come'. Slowly build the distance all the while using the long line.

Before you can try off-leash outdoor you want to introduce the 'let's go' or 'let's play' cue which combines the sit-stay.

Ask him to sit-stay beside you, then use your release cue, 'let's go', and start walking. As he moves away and then moves ahead of you, call him back to you (click on a turn of the head towards you), as he starts coming towards you, you might want to encourage him (I held my arms open), reward him when he gets to you, then ask him to sit (reward).

The last step is to practice off-leash - again, you will do this in a space that is enclosed and where he will be safe. Simply let him wander away from you and then call his to you using your cue. Be exciting and have a treat ready for him. Try and keep his attention on you as he comes to you - make a noise or hold your arms open - you want him to be focused on you.

Don't keep repeating the cue or start raising your voice if he doesn't come. This will confuse him, and he won't be able to understand what his cue word is, eventually tuning it out which means he just won't hear it.

If you raise your voice, he won't think that coming to you is going to be lots of fun. Eventually, it could have the opposite effect, and he won't want to come at all.

USING A CLICKER

Clicker training is useful when you want to mark the correct behavior of your puppy at the exact moment that he starts to respond. If you are doing click-reward then it must always be followed by a reward, but the reward and the timing of the reward varies.

In the beginning, all you need to do is get your puppy used to the click-reward (at the start you will use a treat). Keep repeating click-treat. He doesn't have to do anything at this stage as you are just getting him used to the clicker marker which means a reward is coming.

Slowly reduce the time between the click and the treat and vary the gaps - he will still expect the treat and he will know that it is coming, but that it might not happen right away.

Once he gets good at this, you will be able to click without the treat, and vary the reinforcement by using his favorite toy or a quick game that he likes.

For example, when you call his name and he begins to start coming towards you, you can click so that he knows a reward is coming. It helps to keep him motivated to come all the way back to you in the expectation of a good time when he gets there.

Below is how clicker training fits in to the training as well as how it fit in to recall. If you are training without a clicker just ignore the click-marker.

Recall Summary with the Clicker

The general process for recall training is as follows:

1. Call your dog (use your 'come' cue)
2. When he comes ask him to "Sit" (cue). Take his collar and praise him and reward
3. Release him "Ok Go" (cue)

If you are using a clicker as a marker then the complete process would look like this:

1. Get your puppy to come to you. Start by throwing a treat away from you then throw a treat at your feet. Reward every time your puppy comes back to you for any reason. You can add the click with your clicker to mark as soon as he turns towards you.

2. Add a cue . As your puppy turns towards you, again, this is for any reason, add your recall cue and your click (if you are using a clicker to mark or capture the behavior). The recall cue can be 'come', 'here' or a whistle - either your own whistle or use a plastic one.

3. As you are walking on the leash vary the length. Every time he looks towards you, click and then add the recall cue (and don't forget the reward). Practice at different locations and over different distances before you move to the next step.

4. You will now cue him to look and come to you. With your puppy walking in front of you say (or whistle) your cue, as he turns towards you add the click marker. Practice by varying the distance and the speed the dog is moving away. When he returns to you reward.

5. If you want to add a sit then this is when you will add it to your training. When he arrives back to you use your sit cue to get him to sit. As soon as he sits add a click and then the reward.

6. Add a collar hold. You can train this separately or you can add it into the recall process here. When he has arrived back and sits, lean in and take hold of his collar - as you do this use your clicker to mark then reward.

Once he is good and is succeeding with steps 1 to 6 you can start adding in distractions.

You will start with low-level distractions and build them up to higher-value distractions.

Distractions might be kibble, bread, eggs, cheese, meat, and toys (again in order of least to most favorite).

As he moves towards the distraction e.g., the bread, start your recall cue, and the reward process above (if you are using a clicker just add the click marker). If he fails then reduce the value of the distraction you are tempting him with until he is succeeding.

In terms of what other distractions might be, it doesn't need to be his favourite treats but they are a good place to start. You can then add a dog he knows, a dog he doesn't know (high-value distraction), someone he knows, a group of people, a jogger, a bicycle, an old scent, and the high-value new scent (a squirrel that you have noticed running up a tree).

Try and remember to complete a sequence. Try to always have your dog notice you (click), come to you (encouragement), arrive (treat), sit (treat), collar hold (treat), 'go play' (reward). This is much more rewarding than 'come', treat, end of the game.

By continuing to reward after he comes back to you, by rewarding the sit, collar hold and then releasing with a 'go play' cue, he will have the expectation of more exciting things to come than if the rewards ended with the return cue only.

He also knows that he can return to playing if he comes back to you and also receives all of his rewards. Don't forget that the 'go play' cue is a reward in itself.

This will become even more useful once you start going outdoors to parks and longer walks where there are even more exciting distractions and ones that you are not in control of.

PROOFING

Proofing is when you want to 'prove' that the training has worked and you will need to do this before you let your puppy off-leash.

To do this, you will create distractions and then aim to get him to come to you on cue as you have done above but you are testing once more.

Try and arrange a play-date with at least one other dog and then while he is playing with it (and still on the long-line) call him to you. Make sure you have a very tasty treat and be full of praise when he comes to you.

Once he comes to you and receives his reward he is then released to the cue, such as 'let's go', to play again. As already mentioned, this particular activity is also useful to teach him that coming to you doesn't mean the end of the playtime.

The last step is to practice off-leash - again, you will do this in a space that is enclosed and where he will be safe. Simply let him wander away from you and then call him to you using your cue. Be exciting and have a treat ready for him.

Don't keep repeating the cue if he doesn't come and don't raise your voice to a shout (or scream). This will confuse him and he won't be able to understand what his cue word is. If you raise your voice, he won't think that coming to you is going to be lots of fun, and he won't want to come at all.

If he isn't coming to you as you go through all the training then go back to the long line until you are sure he understands what you are asking him to do.

EMERGENCY STOP

Training for an emergency stop can save your dog's life. It is also quite easy to train especially once you have been working on recall training.

First of all, you will want to use a specific cue. This can be any word but, again, it can only have one meaning. The most common word that is used is 'Stop'.

Begin practice at short distances, gradually building to greater challenges. This command could prevent your puppy from running into traffic or approaching dangerous situations.

To begin with, have your puppy sitting in front of you and have a treat in your hand. If your puppy is not food orientated try using one of his toys.

Take a step back, put your arm in the air as if you are trying to stop the traffic or saying hello to someone who is a distance away. This is important as it is more likely that your emergency stop signal will be visual and not sound-based because your dog is more likely to be a distance away from you.

Raise your arm with the treat in your hand, say the word 'Stop', and then throw the treat over your dog's head towards his rear so that the treat falls behind him or just beside him. You want to make sure that your dog needs to turn around to get the treat.

As he starts to return to you, repeat by putting your arm in the air, saying 'Stop' and throwing another treat over his head. This will force him to stop to turn around to get the treat.

You will notice that he starts to pay attention to you and your hand, which is what you want him to do.

Once he is paying attention, stopping and turning to get the treat as you raise your arm, you can think about increasing the distance of your throw. If there are any problems with the next step return to this previous stage.

Keep throwing the treat a bit further away so that there is a bigger distance between you both, so that when you say 'Stop', put your arm in the air, and throw the treat over his head, he is not close to you. This is how you can build up the long-distance emergency stop.

Try to make sure the treat doesn't land in front of him because you want him to turn around to get the treat. You want him to do this because it stops his forward movement. Keep building up the distance and repeating the exercise.

You want to reach the point where, with your arm in the air, you say Stop, he looks towards you and stops. If he starts to come towards you, go back to the first step and reinforce the Stop when he is right in front of you.

If your dog is a fast learner it may take a few days but this can take a few weeks so just be patient.

The very last step is when you don't throw the treat at the end but, instead, you walk towards him to give him the reward. This is because, if you are in a park and he is far away, you won't be able to throw a treat behind him but you want him to know that a reward is coming.

RECALL: WHAT NOT TO DO

- If your dog does not return to you when you call him simply go and retrieve him and put him on his leash. Don't be angry with him, simply put him on the leash, and move him away from whatever it is that is distracting him. This, in itself, lets him know that coming back is a much better option.
- Don't keep calling the same cue over and over again. For example, if he does not come when you call and you keep repeating the cue louder and louder the cue itself will lose its value and your puppy will simply tune it out as noise. If your cue isn't working then choose a new one and train your puppy to know what it is.
- Don't have only one person training him if he lives with other family members. If your puppy is a family dog then everyone needs to be involved in the training, and everyone needs to use the same cues. Ideally, everyone should be involved in the daily training, even for just a few minutes.
- Never punish your puppy when he fails. This is particularly important with recall (and with separation anxiety). If you get angry with them, or punish them, when they finally return to you after not coming back right away, all they will learn is that coming back to you is not a good experience and that it has negative consequences. It is not fun. All this will do is make his recall worse, not better.

- Don't use the "come" cue if your dog if fully focused on something else and is unlikely to 'hear' you. In this case, use his name to get his attention and to check that he can hear you (does he react by turning slightly towards you or twitch his ear). If he does, then use his "come" cue. If he is far away, you can use a whistle or whistle yourself, and if he can see you use your hand signal.
- Therefore, only use your "come" cue if you think it is likely to succeed. If you call and he does not come, walk to him. Don't give him into trouble or reward him. If he does not 'come' you know he is not fully trained so re-start the training to the point he was succeeding, and build it up again from there.
- Finally, do no use the recall cue for things they might not like doing. For example, don't associate it with a bath, or getting groomed, or having a tick removed if they don't like these things.

WALKING TO HEEL

Like recall, walking to heel on or off-leash is a part of daily life and therefore this, too, is vital training. You will want to build it into his daily training routine and do it 2 or 3 times a day for 5-10 minutes.

Heel-work training is one of those times you want to make sure your puppy is hungry so that the treats can have maximum effect and reward. You might also find that you have to retrace the training slightly more often to ensure he is always successful.

Establish the heel position

The perfect heel position is to have your puppy's head or neck in line with the knee or leg. For ease, you can use his collar as a guide.

Like all training today, you are going to show him what you want him to do, and then you are going to teach him the word that describes what he is doing.

There are two ways you can do this that I have found work well and one shows on-leash and one shows off-leash.

1. Start with your puppy in front of you with the leash around your right-hand wrist while controlling the leash with your left hand. Place your left hand about halfway down his leash towards his collar. Hold a treat in your right hand.

Get his attention by saying his name (or using a squeaky toy) and move your left leg back a step but remain stationary. Use the treat in your right hand to encourage him towards you and into the correct position and, as you do this, move your left leg back into position.

You will encourage him to move in a semi-circle to get into the correct position. As soon as he is in the position you want, mark with a click and a treat. You can then add the signal (I use a point signal) by holding the treat in the same hand that you are using to point down by your side. Once he understands this signal, add the verbal cue heel.

2. Start with your puppy in front of you with a treat in both hands. Hold out your hand and show him the treat in your right hand and then guide him around your back until he can see the other hand with a treat in it. It is this hand (your left had in this example), that will take him to the side of your leg and the final heel position. When he reaches the heel position praise him (or click) and give him his treat. Keep repeating until he understands the behavior.

Once you have done this a few times remove the treat from the hand that starts the movement (but keep doing the same routine) and keep the treat in the hand that guides him into the heel position. You will start to use the empty hand to create a visual cue such as pointing to the side (you can start doing this before you remove the treat).

After he has got the hang of this you can start introducing your verbal cue of 'heel'. Say 'heel' point and he should move behind you into the heel position to get his reward.

Start walking

One important tip with walking to heel is not to constantly hold the treat in front of your dog's nose. It will be tempting but it won't teach him what you need him to learn.

To build movement into his heel-work and walking, bring him to heel while stationary but don't give him the treat right away. Just bring him to heel, and then take a step forward so that he moves with you, and then reward him with his treat. Once he moves with you without hesitation move 2 steps and 3 steps and so on. Don't forget to give him lots of encouragement which will also make him want to look at you.

Every time he walks beside you in the correct position click and praise and reward and slowly build more time (and steps) between the reward. You are aiming to have him happily walking beside you in a straight line with only praise and lots of encouragement.

Once he is walking in a straight line you can then get used to changing direction. You can start to do this in lots of different ways but you can start by simply turning left or right.

Eventually, you will build in the other cues of 'this way' to change direction and his 'sit' cue. For example, you can ask him to sit after walking a few steps or before you change direction. Variations, as you move through his training, will keep him engaged especially as he starts to understand what you want him to do to get his reward.

Keep talking to your puppy and making lots of noises as you do this work - you want him to keep focused and interested in you. This will really help.

As you start walking with your puppy the leash should be relatively loose. If there is tension just stop and wait until the leash slackens then start to walk forward again. This will ensure that he can learn that there is only forward movement when the leash is slack. This works incredibly well.

MEETING OTHER DOGS

One of the most challenging aspects of leash training involves meeting other dogs. Head-on greetings often create tension, as the leash restricts natural greeting behaviors. Instead of allowing direct approaches, teach your puppy to focus on you during passes. Use direction changes and reward calm behavior. A tight leash creates tension, so maintain slack whenever possible.

Sit Stay is one of the most important cues your dog will learn and the ones you will use most often.

You will want to use both verbal and visual cues. Your visual cue for 'stay' will be holding up your hand, but without raising your arm above your head - just hold it in front of you and direct your palm to your puppy's face. This is his visual cue for stay.

The verbal cue would be 'Stay'. Visual cues are also a good way of helping your dog focus on you.

Normally the first part is to ask your puppy to 'sit' then this is followed by 'stay' (or 'wait').

By this stage (by the time you are going for outside walks) you will have trained your puppy to 'sit' and will have practiced some 'stay' in the home or garden. We have covered this earlier.

You will now start to use the sit cue for a variety of reasons. In the car, when you go to the door, when you are at a crosswalk, and so on. This means you need to train him to sit but you also need to let him know when it's okay to move forward.

To do this, start by having him on his leash. Get him to sit (and reward) then decide on your cue for 'let's go' this can be 'let's go' or 'ok go' or whatever you choose. Say your cue and move a few steps and praise him, ask him to sit and reward.

Begin with short distances (a few steps) to get him used to the 'ok go' cue. Repeat the process of 'sit', reward 'ok go' reward, walk a few steps then repeat. This is known as the release cue.

This can mean that the release cue is seen as a reward too because when he comes back he then gets to go and have fun again. It also means that he will learn that coming back doesn't mean the end of the play.

Finally, some trainers consider recall to include holding your puppy's collar when he returns as full recall and they use it before the release cue. The puppy comes back, he sits and the collar is taken then the reward is given. This is followed by the release cue.

Some are happy with only the sit. This really is up to you but I prefer the collar hold as it gives you more control should you ever need it.

In the next section we will review and summarise the release cue and provide some tracking resources and exercises.

11

SEPARATION ANXIETY

Separation anxiety affects at least 1 in 7 dogs in the United States with some studies reporting it might be as high as 1 in 5.

This book is not intended for those dogs with serious anxiety problems, but rather as a guide, to help with some of the basic steps to ease your and your dog's anxiety with separation - and to also explain why they feel the way they do.

Separation training is not generally top of the training list for new puppies - we all know sit, stay, leash and potty training and recall - but it is one of the most important training exercises that needs to be done to make sure you have a happy life with your dog, and one that teaches them that it is okay to be home alone.

Separation Anxiety can be a form of separation distress or isolation distress - a milder form of separation anxiety. I use the terms separation anxiety as a general term but it will depend on the depth of the issue for your dog.

Dogs are used to living with others. They are pack animals, and in nature, are never alone. As mans best friend this means their pack includes us and everyone else we may live within our homes. In its simplest form, being 'separate' is not a natural experience for a dog.

There are a few theories on why dogs react the way that they do but the most important thing to know is that if they are suffering from any degree of separation anxiety then, for one reason or another, they are getting stressed when you leave and they are being left alone. This stress is released in a variety of ways, from whining and barking, to chewing and destruction, as well as bowel release.

All we need to do is to teach them that being alone is not to be feared.

PREPARATION AND SOCIALIZATION

It's a good idea to get your puppy used to being separated from you when they are young. Even if you don't expect to be away from them often, there will be times when you will need to.

Teaching your puppy not to fear this absence, and to let them know that they can be relaxed when you are not there, is one of the best things you can do for both your puppy, and for yourself.

If your puppy can get used to being left for short periods when they are young, then they are more likely to grow up feeling relaxed and comfortable when left on their own for part of the day.

These are all really simple things to do and are obvious once you know them. You will need to do this slowly, teaching them bit by bit over time.

The first 3 basic steps you need to take are the following ones.

1. Pick the room you want your puppy or dog to be in when you are not in the house - either in their basket, bed, or crate. Decide which room this is going to be as early as you can.
2. Once you decide on where this is, start getting them used to

being in this room - don't wait until the time when you are going to leave the house.

3. Spend time with your puppy or dog in this room - you want them to understand it is not a punishment 'place' or a place that is apart from you, but a part of their household.

Create a physical barrier between the room you want them to remain in, and the room you are in - make this something they can see you through (like a gate).

Once you have picked the room that you want your dog to stay in when you leave the house, create a gate to the room but make it a barrier or gate so that your dog can still see you. Remember not to interact with your puppy or dog when they are there - just go about doing things as normal.

Don't forget to spend time with them in this room when you are **not** about to leave, spend time there during the day, or when you are training them so that this becomes a place that you are a part of too.

As you begin their training, the first thing you will do after you have created the gate, is to just be on the other side of the gate to your dog. Do this for 2 or 3 minutes but, if your dog starts to get stressed, just calmly let them out.

Keep building their confidence and slowly make the time longer. Start moving around and doing other things as you build up the time and distance. At this point, you will always be in sight.

If they start to get anxious just move forward or return to the point where they were comfortable. Once they are comfortable with the distance, start to move out of sight to another room for a few minutes, and then repeat the process of stretching the time. Begin by moving to the door of the room.

Then move into another room out of sight (but they will still be able to hear and smell you). Return after a few minutes, and then repeat building up the time as you go along.

Finally, go to the main door and go outside for a few minutes. Once again, repeat the process of increasing the time you are away and check how your dog is reacting.

If there are signs of stress or anxiety just go back a couple of steps and begin building up your dog's confidence once again. Keep the time as short as you need to, it can start with as little as 5 or 10 seconds, and build the time based on your dog's response.

From the very start let the dog know that the place you have chosen is their safe place. Keep all their things in this room and place their bed or crate in here as soon as you can, along with some toys.

If you are using a crate, keep the crate door open - let them get used to going in and out of the crate and choosing to do so.

Get some chew toys for them. Chew toys are good because chewing is calming action (and it's why they chew things they shouldn't). You could also put an item of your clothing in the room so that they can more easily smell you and feel more secure.

The chew toys help your dog use their mind to try and work out how to get the food or treat removed. Giving a reason for dogs to exercise their mind keeps them busy and happily occupied. A Kong is a great chew toy to use because, as well as the chewing, the fun of getting the treats or food out of the inside of the Kong exercises their mind.

Put on some sound - like a radio talk station. Not at a high volume - you only want to muffle any unexpected sounds.

This helps my dogs. I use either the television news or channel that is not likely to have shows with sudden noise but a talk radio station is probably better. Whatever you choose make it something that you listen to so that they are familiar with it.

Your dog will be paying attention to any noise they hear, so this can help disguise some of the day-to-day noises that might go on outside (or inside) your home. It is useful to do this as soon as you begin the training so that it becomes familiar.

Try to teach your dog not to follow you all the time in the home and get them to go to different places in the house. Test them being in a room while you are in another. Don't force this or make them feel stressed about it. You need to teach them to be comfortable with it.

Play a game where you ask them to remain in one room while you move to another, then come back. If they stay where they were, come back and give them a reward - it can be a treat or affection/well done. Once again, do this calmly because if you do, then you will keep your dog calm too.

Remember, when you come back not to increase or cause excitement. This can be a great game for your dog and they will enjoy it as much as you enjoy the results of it.

When you are ready to start the next phase of actually leaving the house there a few more things you can do to keep your dog calm while you are out.

HOW TO LEAVE AND RETURN

Start by leaving the house for a minute, 2 minutes, 3 minutes, and so on, and try and return before they are anxious. If you can, then leave for longer and build up to an hour and so on. If you notice they are not comfortable, then go back to the point when they were, and start from there again. Build the time up again.

Aim to build the routine - perhaps a treat as you leave. But don't kiss and cuddle them and make a fuss with gestures and by your comments. Try and make it as normal and calm as possible.

Of everything I did to help with Barney's separation anxiety, this was the single and most effective technique. It seems so simple yet it seemed to (and still does) calm him. I stopped saying goodbye or paying attention when I left. I just put on my coat, made no fuss at all, and left calmly.

Once you start leaving altogether, do so for short periods at the start if you can, and build up the time to 2, 3 and 4 hours. Do everything as normal and as they are now used to - and make sure they have something to play with or to eat.

Ideally, don't leave your dog alone for more than 4 hours. If you can ask a neighbor or a friend to visit - one your dog might know - or a dog walker. If you are able, come home from work for lunch.

You might start to notice that your dog starts to get anxious when you put on your shoes or coat or if you pick up keys or a bag.

If they start to react to these signs then start training them to get used to these things. Put on your shoes or coat or grab your keys but don't leave. Do something else or sit down and relax (or watch the TV). Keep doing this during the day so that they don't associate these things with your departure.

For example, one of my dogs would start jumping around as soon as I got my boots out. Initially, I put them on in another room, and then I realized I had to be in control of their reaction. I put the boots on then didn't leave (you can do this with keys/coats etc, pick them up or put it on and just sit for a while).

You can also try body-blocking. I used this with the younger dog, Barney (he was more excitable). As soon as he started to get agitated as the boots or coat came out I interrupted his behavior by standing up straight and then asking him to go to his basket. It's important not to be angry - they aren't doing anything wrong - you just want them to do something else so let them know what that is e.g. go to their crate or their basket.

You might need to re-trace your steps a few times, and go back a few paces in the separation training from time-to-time, as you are building their confidence and their sense of 'normal'. Just go back to the point where your dog was last comfortable.

Take this slowly - leave and come back. Build their knowledge and confidence. Having them exercised will help reduce their energy levels so remember to make sure they have had a walk and have been fed. This will make them tired.

You can also try giving them a favorite treat. This might help them associate your departure with something they can look forward to. Someone I know uses a hollowed-out bone with frozen dog food inside (they put the dog food in the bone then freeze it). You could do the same with a Kong.

When you return, don't get them excited with happy cries of "Hello!". Don't over-excite them, or over-reward them when you come back. Just arrive home and then ignore them for 5 minutes. You need to make the exit and return a very normal thing rather than any kind of event to be excited about.

If they have done something wrong on your return don't punish them or shout at them. They won't understand why.

Summary

- Don't make a fuss of your dog when you leave. Don't kiss them and say 'goodbye'.
- Leave calmly.
- Give them their favorite treat as you leave - give them something to chew on.
- Make sure they have been exercised.
- Don't excite them as soon as you return home, wait a few minutes before greeting them.

LEAVING WHEN USING A CRATE

When you put your dog in their crate (if you use a crate) before you leave then don't close the door right away. Put them in and wait until they calm down or lie down.

This might take a few minutes or more so do something else and give them time to relax and be calm. Close and open the door a few times if you like, but wait until they lie down before you close the door.

Don't bribe them into the crate with a treat and then immediately shut the door - just take your time, and let them take their time to get comfortable.

Once they are comfortable in their space and their room then you can start moving away using the methods detailed in the first step.

NOT ALL DOGS ARE THE SAME

Separation or canine separation anxiety can affect all dogs. Although research suggests that dogs are more likely to develop separation behavior problems if they are male, come from a shelter, or are separated from the litter before they are 60 days old.

Separation anxiety can, and does, occur for other reasons. It also happens with puppy's and dogs beyond the puppy stage too.

Dogs that tend to have higher levels of alertness, which are more common in some types of breeds than others, are also thought to increase the chance of that dog experiencing separation anxiety.

Not all dogs of the same breed will develop separation anxiety, it just means that there that they might be more susceptible.

Some examples of these breeds, in no particular order, are:-

- Border Collies are not only highly alert but also very human-focused.
- German and Australian Shepherds due to their high levels of vigilance, energy and loyalty.
- Bichon Frises and Chihuahuas as companion dogs who love sitting around on your lap or getting carried around in your purse. They are used to being with you all the time.
- Cocker Spaniels and King Charles Spaniels, just like the Labrador and Collie, Spaniels have been trained to work with us and strive to make us happy.

In research, mixed breed dogs were more likely to destroy, urinate or defecate when left alone, whereas Wheaten Terriers were likely to vocalize, salivate or pant.

And where separation anxiety existed, almost all of the dogs also had a fear of noise.

CAUSES AND SIGNS OF SEPARATION ANXIETY

Separation anxiety is not a failure on the owner's part, and there can be many reasons that a dog reacts like this.

There may have been a change in ownership either from another home or from a shelter, there may have been a house move or a change in the routine of the family, it might be due to divorce or the loss of a family member (usually another dog but it could be a cat or even a family member moving away to school).

For puppy's, it might simply be the first time they have been left alone having been used to being around people all the time.

If they are already nervous or uncomfortable then they will feel even more vulnerable when they need to deal with these 'threats' alone in their home.

Finally, dogs may be bored. Boredom usually affects young or energetic dogs who still don't know what to do when they are left to play - or relax - alone and they will seek out ways to keep themselves entertained. Like chewing furniture - this is also a calming activity - or exploring the trash. Exercise will help with this.

Dogs will get bored when they are left alone. Your dog will sleep — dogs sleep for between to 10 to 14 hours a day - but he will be awake at various points, and he will be looking for something to do.

He might have a sniff around, have a drink or two, and then look for something else to occupy his mind, his energy, and his time.

Dogs like to put things in their mouth, some things fit in their mouths and some things don't. This means that sometimes the mess you discover on returning home is simply a sign of a bored dog and not necessarily one suffering from anxiety.

This doesn't make the experience of returning home any more pleasant, but exercise will help, and finding toys that he can play with will relieve some of that boredom. Other signs, that are more likely to be separation anxiety, are more obvious.

Dogs will do some of these things some of the time. But when they display this behavior some, or most of the time, then it is likely your dog is suffering from some degree of separation anxiety.

Commonly, the signs of distress will begin almost as soon as you leave the house.

Howling or barking is not the only sign of separation anxiety. Other signs are excessive barking, panting or whining, and indoor accidents. This won't be due to not being housebroken.

Stress can result in either peeing or pooping or both. They may also chew things to calm themselves, scratch at doors or windows and some might try to escape.

They are more likely to be scratching the door that you left from, or the window from where they can see you leave, they might chew something that smells of you - a shoe, sock, or even a magazine.

Signs of general stress in dogs will be panting and pacing and this may well be evident in your dog if he or she is suffering from separation anxiety.

Is your dog panting when you return home? This might be due to whining and barking while you were gone. You will notice this at other times too.

Separation anxiety is not only when you leave the house and the dog is alone. It can also be when dogs become anxious when they are not seated near you or can't see you even if you are still at home.

Does your dog follow you around and want to sit beside you all the time? Do they sit against your legs or feet (this way they will know as soon as you move)?

What happens when you leave? Is it only you that your dog is focused on (if you share your home with family). In some cases, it doesn't matter if the dog is with another person in the home when you leave.

If you share your home and want to find this out, simply have a friend or another family member stay with your dog (with some treats) and leave the house. How does your dog react? Do they ignore the treats and look for you and if they do, how long for? Or do they settle down with the other person and enjoy their treats?

If you are not sure how your dog is reacting when you leave then it is useful to record your dog when you are not there. What does he do when you leave? Does he go to the door for a few minutes - how long? Take note of everything you can see and what he does. This is one of the best ways to find out what is happening when you are gone.

WHAT TO WATCH OUT FOR

Does your dog start to behave differently as you get ready to leave, either before you have started to get ready or when you are getting ready to leave? My dogs started to react to me picking up my coat or my car keys. If I was going on a trip - which might only be once every few months, one of my dogs would immediately start to pace around and look 'sad' as soon as I got a suitcase out.

The first thing to do is to take notice of their behavior and try and think about if it has changed and why it might have changed. What changes have you made, if any?

Notice how much and how often your dog is following you (even if he is a new puppy). If it's an older dog try to think back to any changes - is he sitting beside you more often, following your more than he used to? Is there any other reason or a point in time that you can identify?

The solution to this part of their behavior is to slowly build them up to being comfortable with you not being beside or near them so that they get used to your absence and learn (or re-learn) that you come back.

It is perfectly natural for dogs to show some anxiety - so don't over-react or worry about it. But if they do suffer from anxiety or nervousness, it is more likely they will also suffer from separation anxiety.

Sometimes any or some of the signs can be there for other reasons so if you are worried at all just check with your veterinarian.

WHY PUNISHMENT WON'T WORK

Before we talk about all the things that can be done to help with separation anxiety, it is useful to understand why punishment just won't work.

Have you ever taken your dog over to the 'scene of the crime' and pointed at it? I have done this and we all will have done this.

Notice that the dog appears to look guilty and might cower. We, as humans, project our feelings or interpretation onto this behavior, and assume that the dog is noticing what it has done and feels 'guilty' about it.

This is not what is happening. What we see as 'looking guilty' is appeasement behavior. It can be a way that your dog is releasing tension to try and get rid of their fear. The cowering, flat ears and tail between the legs, or looking away, is your dog trying to placate you.

The dog will know that she emptied the trash all over the kitchen floor and dragged some of it into other rooms, but it won't connect what it has done wrong.

And he definitely won't connect something that happened 2 or 3 hours ago when you arrive home to find the mess.

All your dog will know is that you are not happy and he will pick this up from you and be fearful, and will try to placate you but he won't know what he has done. He only knows that you are unhappy right now. No matter how much you point at that mess your dog is not going know why you are angry.

Dogs won't associate something done hours or even minutes ago with the here-and-now. No matter how much we tell them, they simply won't understand why we are angry with them - just that we are.

And this means they won't understand why they are being punished. They will only connect that you arrive home and they get punished.

This all means that punishment when you return home will make your dog not only stressed about you leaving, but stressed about you coming home too. This can make any anxiety worse.

Just remember, the dog has not done this to deliberately annoy you nor to 'get back' at you. Dogs just don't think like that. They did it because they were stressed and anxious or bored and they tried to use that pent-up energy.

They might look 'guilty' when you return because they have learned that they got into trouble the last time you came back - so they appease you as soon as you return.

But they are doing this because when you return, they sometimes get punished, so they react to prevent it as much as they can.

SOME OTHER USEFUL TIPS

1. Exercise is an important part of curing separation anxiety.

A 2015 study by PLoS One found that dogs with noise sensitivity and separation anxiety had less daily exercise.

This suggests that exercise is one of the biggest things you can do to prevent or improve separation anxiety in your dog.

You need to make sure your pet gets lots of exercise every day because a tired, happy dog will be less stressed when you leave.

The study also found that dogs that were exercised off-leash were less likely to suffer from separation anxiety or fear around noise. The likely reason for this is that being on a leash, partly on a leash, or running free, has an impact on the amount of exercise a dog has.

2. A dog whines when it starts to get tense or excited. Sometimes they whine because they want something - if this is the case, they will make it obvious what they want. If you notice this and the reason is not obvious then try and work out why it might be excited and calm them down before the excitement level rises.

3. If you have multiple household members then try and share the dog

equally amongst everyone so the dog doesn't focus all their attention onto one person.

THE 10 STEPS TO HELP SEPARATION ANXIETY

1. Create a physical barrier between the room you want them to remain in and the room you are in - make this something they can see you through.
2. Put their bedding or basket in this room along with any of their toys and the bowls.
3. Put on some sound - like a radio talk station. Not at a high volume - you only want to muffle any unexpected sounds.
4. Teach your dog not to follow you all the time in the home.
5. Don't make a fuss of your dog when you leave. Don't cuddle and kiss them and say 'goodbye'
6. Leave calmly
7. Give them their favorite treat as you leave - give them something to chew on
8. Make sure they have been exercised
9. When you return don't over-excite your dog as soon as you arrive home (if there is a mess, don't punish your dog)
10. Wait a few minutes before you acknowledge them and say hello.

12

CONCLUSION

The intention of this book is to be as practical and useful as possible to new puppy owners - even those who may have raised a pup before and who may have forgotten some of the training tips.

By now you will be noticing your how your puppy's behaves and how he responds to different cues and distractions as well as what his most favourite treats are - knowing this will be a gold mine., especially if you have been able to work out how he ranks them. And try to do this with toys too. It will all help with the times you need to leave him for a few hours aiding any signs of separation anxiety.

Even if you don't fill out all the tables, be sure to read them because they will prompt you to consider what you are teaching and what your pup is learning.

A puppy is a wonderful thing and they grow into loving friends and companions - one's that you will love dearly for a very long time.

Enjoy the journey - and take lots of pictures!

Before I go, if you found this book useful I would love it if you could leave a review.

Helen

13
TOXIC PLANTS AND FOOD

PLANTS AND YOUR GARDEN

The BlueCross provide the following information on which plants are toxic for our pups. While some will only cause a tummy upset some are more dangerous. Most dogs will avoid toxic plants, but puppies are more likely to explore and eat things they are not supposed to be consuming!

Although the following are known to be toxic, they will usually only cause mild symptoms but you want to avoid your puppy eating too much in a short time.

- Autumn crocus (Colchicum autumnale)
- Azalea/rhododendrons (Rhododendron species)
- Bluebells (Hyacinthoides species)
- Common poppy (Papaver rhoeas)
- Cotoneaster (Cotoneaster species)
- Crocuses (Crocus species)
- Daffodils (Narcissus species)

- Dumbcane (Diffenbachia species)
- Foxgloves (Digitalis species)
- Garden star-of-Bethlehem (Ornithogalum umbellatum)
- Grape vine fruits (Vitis vinifera)
- Giant hogweed (Heracleum mantegazzianum)
- Holly (Ilex aquifolium)
- Hyaciniths (Hyacinthus orientalis)
- Ivy (Hedera helix)
- Laburnum (Laburnum anagyroides)
- Lily of the valley (Convallaria majalis)
- Mistletoe (viscum Album)
- Onion and garlic plants (Allium species)
- Oleander (Nerium oleander)
- Potato plants (Solanum tuberosum)
- Pieris plants (Pieris species)
- Rowan (Sorbus aucuparia)
- Snowdrops (Galanthus)
- Tulips (Tulipa species)
- Yew (Taxus species)

Not all parts of these plants are toxic and sometimes only the bulbs or berries will cause problems, but it's always safer to keep your dog away from the whole plant.

SYMPTOMS OF PLANT POISONING

- Drooling
- Not eating
- Low energy
- Vomiting or diarrhoea – especially if it contains bits of chewed up plants
- Drinking or weeing more
- Rashes and red, irritated skin

- Mouth ulcers and pale gums
- Twitching or seizures
- Collapse

If your dog eats a poisonous plant or is showing any signs of toxicity, call your vet immediately.

OTHER GARDEN HAZARDS

Compost and grass clippings - these can contain dangerous moulds or bacteria.

Fungi and mushrooms - not all types of fungi are dangerous, but some can be life-threatening if your dog eats them. So it's best to avoid them completely.

Pesticides, weed killers and fertilisers - avoid spraying any areas your dog usually visits and keep pets out of any areas that you need to treat.

Grass seeds - these are often in fields of long grass and they can get lodged in your dog's skin, especially in their paws, armpits and ears where they can cause irritation and infection.

DANGEROUS FOODS

Some common human foods can cause anything from mild digestive issues to severe, life-threatening conditions in dogs. Here's a list of the most common human foods that we might not think about, including how much is considered dangerous:

1. Alcohol

Why it's dangerous: Alcohol can cause ethanol poisoning, leading to slowed breathing, decreased heart rate, vomiting, tremors, coma, or death.

How much is dangerous: Even small amounts (a few licks) can cause poisoning in dogs. Never give alcohol to your dog, and keep beverages like beer, wine, and spirits well out of reach.

2. Chocolate and Cocoa

Why it's dangerous: Chocolate contains theobromine and caffeine, which are toxic to dogs. Theobromine affects the heart, kidneys, lungs, and nervous system.

How much is dangerous: The darker the chocolate, the more dangerous it is. For example:

- Milk chocolate: 1 ounce per pound of body weight can be toxic.
- Dark chocolate: As little as 0.1 ounces per pound of body weight can cause symptoms.
- Baking chocolate: Even smaller amounts (0.1 ounce for a 20-pound dog) can be fatal.

A medium size dog can be affected by just 6 small squares of baking chocolate, but it would take nearly ¾ lb. of milk chocolate to have the same affect. If your puppy or dog has eaten dark chocolate contact your vet immediately. You will be asked the weight of your dog so its useful to always check his weight regularly. Symptoms include seizures, vomiting, diarrhoea, excitement, tremors, abnormal heart rate/rhythm, staggering, and even coma.

3. Caffeine

Why it's dangerous: Caffeine, found in coffee, tea, energy drinks, and some chocolates, affects the central nervous system and heart, leading to restlessness, rapid heart rate, vomiting, and potentially death.

How much is dangerous: Ingesting even a small amount, such as from coffee grounds or tea bags, can cause symptoms. Dogs can be seriously affected by 150 mg of caffeine per kilogram of body weight (equivalent to around 2 teaspoons of instant coffee for a 10-pound dog).

4. Grapes and Raisins

Why they're dangerous: Grapes and raisins can cause kidney failure in dogs, though the exact toxin is still unknown.

This also includes other dried variants like sultanas and currants and any foods containing grape, such as grape juice, raisin cereal, raisin bread, granola, trail mix, and raisin cookies or bars. Early signs are vomiting, diarrhoea, and lethargy. One of the most common causes is from your dog eating wild bird food. Ground feeders should be enclosed which only allow birds to enter.

How much is dangerous: Even small amounts can be toxic, with as little as a few grapes or raisins potentially causing kidney damage in dogs. If your dog ingests any amount, seek veterinary care immediately.

5. Onions, Garlic, and Chives

Why they're dangerous: These foods contain thiosulfate, which can cause the destruction of red blood cells, leading to anemia and dogs don't have the liver enzyme necessary to digest it. The amount required will depend on body weight. It is toxic in raw, cooked or dried form

How much is dangerous: Eating just 0.5% of your dog's body weight in onions or garlic can cause toxicity. For example, around 50 grams (1.75 ounces) of onion can be toxic to a 10-pound dog.

6. Macadamia Nuts

Why they're dangerous: Macadamia nuts can cause weakness, vomiting, hyperthermia (fever), and tremors.

How much is dangerous: Toxicity has been reported with as little as 2.4 grams per kilogram of body weight. Even a few nuts can cause symptoms in small dogs.

7. Xylitol (Artificial Sweetener)

Why it's dangerous: Xylitol causes a rapid release of insulin, leading to hypoglycemia (low blood sugar), seizures, liver failure, and even death.

Xylitol is used as a sweetener in several products including candy, gum, baked goods, diet foods, and even some peanut butter and toothpaste.

How much is dangerous: As little as 0.1 grams per kilogram of body weight can cause hypoglycemia. For a small dog, this can mean a single piece of sugar-free gum.

8. Avocado (Persin)

Why it's dangerous: Avocados contain persin, which can cause vomiting, diarrhea, and heart congestion in dogs.

How much is dangerous: While the flesh of the avocado is less toxic, the pit, leaves, and bark contain high amounts of persin. Ingesting any part of the avocado plant can lead to toxicity.

9. Raw Potato and Unripe Tomatoes

Why they're dangerous: Potatoes and tomatoes contain solanine, a toxin that can cause gastrointestinal issues, lethargy, and neurological symptoms. Solanin (and tomatin) in particularly found in the green parts of the tomato plant (leaves, stems, of unripe tomatoes). Ripe tomatoes are generally considered safe for dogs in small amounts .

Raw Potato's also contain solanine which is mainly found in green or sprouted potatoes. Cooking potatoes reduces the solanine content, making them safe for dogs to eat in moderation when fully cooked.

It can cause serious symptoms like vomiting, diarrhea, lethargy, and confusion in high doses.

How much is dangerous: While small amounts may not be fatal, ingestion of large quantities can be toxic, especially if the potatoes are raw or the tomatoes unripe.

10. Bones

Why they're dangerous: Cooked bones, in particular, can splinter and cause choking, internal blockages, or punctures in the digestive tract.

How much is dangerous: Any cooked bone is a hazard. Raw bones can be safer but should always be given under supervision to avoid choking.

11. Nuts (Pecans, Almonds, Walnuts) and Cherry, peach, apricot and plum stones

The pits (stones) of **cherries, peaches, apricots, and plums** naturally contain amygdalin, which can release cyanide when chewed or broken. Cyanide poisoning in dogs can cause symptoms such as vomiting, labored breathing, dilated pupils, rapid heart rate (tachycardia), cardiac arrhythmias, and eventually coma. Urgent veterinary treatment is essential if cyanide poisoning is suspected, as it can be life-threatening.

In addition the leaves, fruit, seeds and bark of avocados contain Persin, which will cause vomiting and diarrhoea. (**Pecans, Almonds, Walnuts, Macadamia**) - these have the potential to not only cause vomiting but possible pancreatitis. Walnuts, especially moldy ones, can cause tremors and seizures.

How much is dangerous: Even a small handful of nuts can cause gastrointestinal distress or more serious symptoms in dogs.

12. Coconut

Coconut flesh and coconut oil are not toxic to dogs but may cause stomach upset or diarrhea if consumed in large quantities. Coconut water, however, should not be given to dogs because it contains high levels of potassium, which can lead to hyperkalemia and potential heart issues.

13. Shellfish

Some dogs may be sensitive or allergic to shellfish (such as prawns or langoustine), causing vomiting, diarrhea, or other reactions even with small amounts and one of my own dogs has a severe reaction to prawns. While shellfish can cause issues for some dogs, fish is generally safe and even beneficial when cooked properly. Fish is a good source of protein and omega-3 fatty acids, but it should always be cooked thoroughly and cooled to avoid parasites and bacteria, and any bones should be removed.

WHAT TO DO IF YOUR PET IS POISONED

These are the instructions from the Pet Poison helpline:-

1. **Remove your pet from the area** where the potential poisoning occurred to prevent further exposure.

2. **Check your pet's condition** to ensure they are safe, breathing normally, and not showing signs of immediate distress.
3. **Do NOT give any home antidotes** (such as hydrogen peroxide) without professional advice.
4. **Do NOT induce vomiting** unless instructed to do so by a veterinarian or the Pet Poison Helpline. Inducing vomiting can sometimes make the situation worse, depending on the substance ingested.
5. **Contact your veterinarian or the Pet Poison Helpline immediately** for guidance. In the U.S., you can call the Pet Poison Helpline.
6. **If veterinary attention is necessary,** go to your nearest veterinarian or emergency clinic immediately.

14

VACCINATIONS AND BREEDER

VACCINATIONS

First Vaccination (Date and details):

_____

Second Vaccination (Date and details):

_____

ELECTRONIC TAGS

If you puppy is electronically tagged take a note of the company used and the identifier for you puppy.

Name:

_____

Identifier:

_____

BREEDER AND BREED HISTORY

Breeder Name:

_____

Breeder Contact Details:

_____

_____

Write down any history of the puppy's breed line that you received from the breeder (and that you might forget later).

_____

_____

_____

_____

_____

15
FREE DOG TRAINING WORKSHOP

Our friends at the K9 Training Institute are conducting a free online workshop on how to use hand signals and how to get your dog to become as well-behaved as a service dog, You can sign up by using the QR code at the end.

If You Own a Dog, Or Are Just About to Get One, This is For You

Training a dog is certainly the hardest part of owning a dog. It can be very frustrating having a dog that is not housebroken, or barks excessively, or keeps pulling on the leash during your walks, or doesn't respond whenever it's called, or jumps up on people, etc.

You'll be fed up, because it's pretty exhausting to keep trying to make them listen. You'll wonder how professional dog trainers help dogs behave exactly the way they (the trainers) want them to.

But hiring a trainer can be quite expensive, and to be honest, you don't really need to.

I'll explain how in a minute. First, let me talk about WHY your dog seems to be so hard to train.

Most people start training their dogs using verbal cues or commands like SIT, STAY, etc. Because that's what we have been taught to do.

Here's the problem - that might be exactly how NOT to train a dog!

Why?

Because the science of animal behavior says that starting your training using only verbal cues sets your dog up for failure.

Dogs that are trained only using verbal cues never get trained properly. Or at least, the training doesn't last long.

So what's the best way to train a dog?

The science is very clear on this - dogs are best trained by using body language. Now, this doesn't mean that you should never use verbal cues. What it means is that you should always START your dog's training using body language as well as a verbal cue to reinforce your dog's training.

So how do you train your dog using body language?

I just came across this fantastic free workshop from the K9 Training Institutethat helps you learn how to do just that.

The workshop is designed to help "normal" dogs like yours have the same level of calmness, obedience and impulse control as service dogs.

It's being conducted by Dr. Alexa Diaz (one of the top service dog trainers in the U.S.) and Eric Presnall (host of the hit Animal Planet TV show "Who Let the Dogs Out").

The techniques described in the workshop are fairly groundbreaking - I haven't seen anyone else talk of these techniques.

This is because it's the first time ever (at least that I know of) that anyone has revealed the secret techniques used by the service dog training industry to train service dogs.

In the free workshop, you'll discover:

1. How to train your dog using body language, rather than verbal cues
2. The 3 key techniques that service dog trainers use to train dogs, and how you can use them too
3. The most important step that "normal" dog owners have been missing (this is very important to get your dog's attention, and it works 100% of the time)
4. How to stop bad behaviors like excessive barking, pulling on the leash, jumping, etc.
5. Why a lot of dog owners are unable to establish the amazing bond that service dog trainers have with their dogs

etc.

The tips shared in this free workshop work on ALL dog breeds - from small breeds like Pomeranians and Chihuahuas to large breeds like English Mastiffs and Great Danes.

Also, puppies as young as 6 weeks old, and previously untrained adult dogs as old as 13 years, have been successfully trained using these techniques.

It's not a live workshop - rather, it's a pre-recorded workshop, which means that you can watch it at your convenience.

However, while the workshop is free, I am not sure whether it's going to be online for too long, so please check it out as soon as you can. The QR code is on the next page.

QR CODE

Printed in Dunstable, United Kingdom

66974031R00090